A WEEK IN VENICE

NCQ TITLES

Legal Fictions
Politics & Letters
On Yeats: Upon a House
Drama & Democracy
Locating Theology

Time Pieces
Critical Paranoia
On Joyce: 3 easy essays
On Eliot
Literary Conversions

Film-texts

A Trip to Rome
A Short Break in Budapest
Magic in Prague
WWW: the weekend that warped the world

A Week in Venice
Four Days in Athens
The Last Priest of Horus

Play-texts

Darwin: an evolutionary entertainment
Strange Meetings & Shorts

Eliotics

Forthcoming

Rubbishing Hockney & other reviews
On Collecting Walter Benjamin
Autobiography & Class Consciousness
Considering Canterbury Cathedral

Though each can be read independently,
these NCQ publications, taken together,
comprise a single hyper-text collection.

A WEEK IN VENICE

a film-text

Bernard Sharratt

New Crisis Quarterly
2015

NEW CRISIS QUARTERLY

ncq@newcrisisquarterly.myzen.co.uk

First published 2015

ISBN : 978-1-910956-14-4

For
Marion, Nicola, & Paul
with love and thanks for
my 70th birthday
in Venice

This film-text is not written with actual film production in mind. Though it plays with a variety of film genres, it is primarily intended to be read—and imagined.

Venice is an appropriate place as the setting for my characters and my themes, and the script is designed to be easily supplemented by on-line images and maps of the specified sites and scenes. Other film-texts in this 'city' series are set in Athens, Prague, Rome, and Budapest, and the series will probably conclude with *A Last Sight of Europe*.

A film-text is a particularly suitable form for the New Crisis Quarterly imprint, since that name revives the title of a very short-lived periodical whose first, only, and final issue appeared in 1984, under the guise of my *The Literary Labyrinth*. Its editorial programme was to publish reviews of imagined books I didn't feel I had the time actually to write, so its readers were cheerfully invited, if so inclined, to write those works themselves. In the same spirit, reading a film-text means that most of the work of imagining the film can be done by you, which is part of the fun of writing them.

B.S.
2015

FADE IN [TITLE OVER:]

*View from aircraft circling over and flying into
Venice Airport in glorious sunset, rapidly fading into
darkness as the aircraft lands.*

WRITTEN:] Day One: Tuesday

1. INT. VENICE AIRPORT ARRIVALS.

*DAVE and KATE are next to each other in a queue
shuffling towards immigration control.
It is 9.30 pm. Everybody looks tired and fed up.*

*Dave is perhaps mid-thirties, probably a
businessman. Kate is late twenties, attractive, but not
easy to categorise. They don't know each other.*

> PA ANNOUNCEMENT
> British Airways once again apologises for the
> long delay in the arrival of Flight 8566, due to
> the on-board illness of a passenger and the
> emergency diversion to Geneva. We sincerely
> hope that you have not been too severely
> inconvenienced and that you will fly with us
> again.

> DAVE
> *(mutters)* Maybe. Not. *(turns to Kate)* 'Not
> too severely inconvenienced', indeed—only
> the worst airport in Europe at which to arrive
> this late.

KATE
(hesitates to respond, then:) How so?

DAVE
Getting a vaporetto, at this hour — it's now
the bus or a damned expensive water taxi —
(looks at watch) though we might just make
the last Alilaguna service—

KATE
I haven't a clue what you're talking about—
I'm afraid it's my first visit to Venice.

DAVE
Sorry —er, David Hutton *(offers handshake,
ignored)* —well, the problem is, it's now
either a ride across the water, which is great
— but the last regular service goes in *(checks
watch)* 22 minutes—or a pretty grotty bus ride
along the land route and over the bridge—
and that's certainly not the way you want to
see Venice for the first time. Where are you
staying? Mestre? Or in Venice proper?

KATE
Er, it's near the Zattere *[Za-TER-re]*
vaporetto station, according to my map at
least —*(reluctantly offers her hand* —Kate—
so what's this other service you mentioned?

DAVE
It's a private ferry line but reasonable cost—
unlike the taxis—if you trust me, follow me
close when we get through passport control—
got any more luggage to collect? And can you
run, or walk fast??

                    KATE
          Just this bag—and I'll keep up. Don't worry.

                    DAVE
          Right—you're on. I'll grab a trolley if I can.
          I'll get you there—and it's ZA-terre, by the
          way.

2. EXT. COVERED WALKWAY.

[CREDITS AND JAUNTY MUSIC OVER:]

*Exuberant tracking shots of the long covered walk
from the airport to the Alilaguna landing bay as
Dave and Kate race along it, wildly pushing a trolley
with their baggage, in what becomes a high spirited
dash—They just make it in time to buy tickets and
tumble aboard the last boat as it begins to leave the
dock.*

3. INT. BOAT.

*From inside the boat only dark waters and far lights
are visible. Both have sobered down. Kate is wary.*

                    DAVE
          Well, it's a shame you can't actually *see*
          much—it's a pretty spectacular ride—but do
          come back this way, especially at sunset.

*No response from Kate, who looks through the dark
windows at lights and reflections.*

DAVE
(tries again) Better than a bus in any case!
(no response) Unfortunately, this isn't the
route that goes all the way round to Zattere,
so let's work out the best way to get you there.
What's the address you need to get to?

KATE
(hesitates, then:) The Hotel Calcina.

DAVE
Ah, Ruskin's old place. Good choice. OK,
let's see. Simplest to get off at Fondamente
Nuove—no, Sant' Alvise is better, and if we
then walk through to Marcuola, I can drop my
bag en route, and then take you on the N line
to Accademia—right down the Grand Canal
—which *is* a great way to see the place for the
very first time, after all.

KATE
(just refraining from a complete put-down)
Sounds like I'm taking you out of your way.
Perhaps you'd better just show me on the map.

DAVE
Well, OK—maps out—but I really don't
mind. I love that ride down the Grand Canal
anyway. No trouble at all. And finding the
Calcina might be a bit tricky for you—er, for
anyone strange to the place, I mean.

KATE *(relents a little)*
Fine. You know Venice well?

                    DAVE
I come here every chance I get. I'm in
insurance. And we have quite a few blue chip
clients here, so—

                    KATE
Insurance. I see.
(She looks pointedly out of the window.)

4. EXT. CANNAREGIO STREETS.

They disembark. And walk through Cannaregio.
Each pulling luggage on wheels.

                    DAVE
This is the old Ghetto area—Not the best time
to *arrive* in Venice—most places have closed
by now—but the best time to *walk* in
Venice—after all the day-trippers have
gone—enjoy the peace and quiet. Pity about
the rattle of the wheels though!

5. EXT. AT DOOR OF HOTEL LEONARDO.

                    DAVE
Just hang on here a mo', Kate. I'll let them
know I've finally got here, dump my bag.
Only be a sec.

Kate waits, resisting the urge to tell him to sod off.
Dave comes out to her.

                    DAVE
Right, I'll take your bag now if you like.
We're heading for the Marcuola vaporetto
station. Five minute walk —if you've got a

mobile better tell the Calcina you're finally on your way. Take us about thirty minutes. OK?

6. EXT. STREETS.

They walk across Rio Terra San Leonardo, towards the Marcuola ferry stage. As they turn a corner, they see a small fire against the wall of the closed public toilets. A couple of policemen and some firemen are putting out the flames. They are directed to go down another street to the vaporetto station.

> DAVE
>
> My word, we can't have *that* burn down. Irreplaceable! —there are only six public toilets in the whole of Venice!

Kate is not very amused.

7. EXT. ON A VAPORETTO. THE GRAND CANAL.

Dave tries to make conversation.
Kate is not responsive.

> DAVE
> Isn't it magnificent!

> KATE
> Marvellous.
> *(pause)*
> I think I just want to look at it, thank you.

8. EXT. MOONLIGHT. FONDAMENTO ZATTERE PONTO LUNGO.

> DAVE
> Look, are you sure I can't take you off to dinner or a bite somewhere. It's pretty hard to find a place to eat at this hour.

They are passing two fish restaurants which are clearly still open. Kate glances pointedly at them.

> DAVE
> They will have finished serving an hour ago. Believe me.

> KATE
> *(Calls to a waiter clearing up.*
> *In confident Italian.)*
> Sei ancora servire? i pasti?
> [Are you still serving food?]

> WAITER
> No, no, signorina. Last orders, hour ago.

> DAVE
> *(modestly ironic cough)* OK, just one tip about eating in Venice. It can be a drag, pretty expensive, and often not very good. What I do is just buy a baguette, some ham, cheese, whatever, and eat it wherever. At the far end of this, the Fondamenta Zattere, is a decent little supermarket, tucked away, but it's good —and the nicest place around here just to sit in the shade is the gardens of the Casa Rezzonico. Best lunch in Venice. Well, sort of.

KATE
Thanks. I'll remember it.

9. EXT. OUTSIDE HOTEL CALCINA.

KATE
Thank you again—a great introduction to
Venice. I'll be fine here.

DAVE *(hands her a card)*
There's my mobile number if I can be useful.
(hesitates) Well, enjoy Venice! Ciao, Kate.

KATE
Goodbye, David.

10. EXT. FONDAMENTA ZATTERE.

Dave walks away. To himself:

DAVE
Worth a try. Ah well. Now to work.

*As he walks he makes a call on his mobile. He now
speaks in a quite different tone, sharp, business-like:*

Fabrizio? It's David, yes. Sorry. Flight was
delayed. Thought you might still be
working, though. *(pause)* Yes. So, they took
out all six? I was actually passing one, near
Marcuola. So that's number two : 'servizio
pubblico'—si? Well, we don't insure toilets
—I think. Shall I leave it till tomorrow? See
what you've got by then. *(pause)* OK, at ten.
Your San Marco office. Yes. Oh, hang on.

Can you check something for me. Passenger on the 8566 flight, staying at Hotel Calcina. First name, Kate. Can you just check the lists and get her surname for me. *(pause)* Yes I know you really shouldn't. Just a favour. *(pause)* No, not work. Just, er, interested. Come on, Fabrizio, you know I could easily get it myself—you're just saving me a tiny bit of legwork. Come on, old friend. *(pause)* OK, tell me tomorrow if you can.

11. INT. HOTEL BEDROOM.

Kate is looking out from her balcony at the waters of the Guidecca Canal

> KATE *(to herself)*
> Right, let's get settled in.

She boots up her laptop and finds an internet connection.

That's fine. Security OK? Yup.

Pauses and ponders a moment. Then starts a rapid search. Commenting to herself:

Let's see if you might be useful after all, Mr David Hutton. Mmm, lots of David Huttons. *(several clicks)* Ah, that's the one. Mmmm. Lloyds of London. Well, well. Very interesting. You know, I might just take your bait. Lunch at Casa Rezzonico. But first—

WRITTEN:] Day Two: Wednesday

12. INT. LARGE OFFICE. MORNING.

A fairly dilapidated but once impressive room.
A working office. Computer. Desk. Chairs.
Large wall map of Venice.
Projector screen connected to computer.

FABRIZIO is about 45, a seasoned and senior
detective in the Venice police.

On the large wall-screen is projected a scan of a
letter. Dave and Fabrizio are standing, looking at it.
The letter, computer printed, is as follows:

Bersagli

1. avviso
2. servizio pubblica
3. sotto gli archi
4. potenza lascia
5. più bella illusione ottica
6. 1911
7. incensato —

è necessario rispondere alle nostre esigenze o si
perde ciò che di valore più
Matteo 14:28   Luca 23:37
Giovanni 1:25   Genesi 13:9

They sit contemplating it for a while.

> DAVE
> Well, I'm not much wiser, now I've actually
> seen it. At least we know what the first two
> targets are, but still no demands yet, I take it.

                    FABRIZIO
But you can see why I alerted you, David.

                    DAVE
Absolutely. Let's see the footage again.
I saw the clips on YouTube, but it's difficult
to make out details.

                    FABRIZIO
The fire service only got there after they'd
started to burn. So here's the best we can
compile at present.

*Projected onto the wall-screen are a few moments of
silent video footage, edited in segments, with
variations of the same scene, which show several
huge commercial advertisements on the frontage of
buildings in the St Mark's area, first beginning to
burn, then being rapidly extinguished.*

                    DAVE
Well, you were dead right to call me.
I checked. We do insure those advertising
hoardings, but only as part of the overall
buildings insurance. And the adverts
themselves are obviously peanuts compared
with what it *might* have cost us if the
buildings themselves had caught fire. But it's
worrying. If it was negligence, we might not
pay out, but that looks pretty deliberate.

                    FABRIZIO
Yes. We think it was acid thrown onto the
fabric of the adverts. It would eat through and
then start to burn. But that kind of fabric is

designed to burn itself out before the
buildings are really threatened.

            DAVE
  How do you throw acid that high?

            FABRIZIO
  A fragile container shot from a catapult?
  Burst on impact? Perhaps.

            DAVE
  And now, after last night's toilet fires, well—
  are we just dealing with some crazy arsonist
  or what? Have you got anything else to go
  on?

            FABRIZIO
  Blank. But I'm pretty sure it's another ransom
  scam, as with the Botticelli two years ago.
  So I was hoping you might have some fresh
  ideas. If it is like that one, it'll be your firm
  paying out.

            DAVE
  Probably. Can I see that letter again?

It comes up on the wall screen.

            DAVE
  Whoever it is, they're obviously a bit different
  from the last lot,anyway. Got a sense of
  humour, even. The first *—avviso—*a
  warning—but it can also mean advert,
  pubblicità, yes?—and then those adverts go
  up in flames. And it promptly gets advertised
  itself on the internet—no self-respecting

tourist could resist putting footage of that
little fire up on YouTube. Of course, nobody
liked those grotesque adverts anyway,
plastered all over the finest buildings in
Venice. So it can be put down to just
disgruntled Venetians making a point. And
whoever did it has definitely made their point.
Then *servizio pubblico*—which would
normally mean civil service, or public utility,
yes?—I don't think you would have reckoned
on them setting fire to toilets! And next,
assuming they're in order: *sotto gli archi*—
underneath the arches—and think how many
arches are there in Venice!

FABRIZIO
Well, it could mean one of the bridges across
the Grand Canal—in which case we only have
three to protect. But it could mean any one of
over four hundred smaller bridges—and it
may not even mean a bridge, but just an
archway. So how do we guard against an
arsonist attacking the arches in Venice,
of all places?

DAVE
Well, what about the rest: *(reads aloud)*
4. potenza lascia
5. più bella illusione ottica
6. 1911
7. incensato —
È necessario rispondere alle nostre esigenze o
si perde ciò che di valore più.
What the hell does *potenza lascia* mean —
power lacks, power leaves? 1911 is the most

worrying, presumably a version of 9/11. But
are there any twin towers in Venice?

FABRIZIO
A Venetian wouldn't have a problem with
either of those questions. *Potenza lascia* is the
first words of the old rule : *Potenza lascia il
posto a vela regola*—power gives way to
sail—a powered boat has to yield to a sailing
boat. Everybody brought up in Venice knows
that—and we have to enforce it, after all. But
what it means here, I have no idea. As for
1911—well, there is *one* tower which dates to
around 1911—

DAVE
Of course, the campanile, rebuilt after the
1902 collapse. Finished in 1911, 1912?
Wow, that's a *big* target. Are they going to
smash a plane into the campanile at St
Mark's? We do *not* insure that, I hope.

FABRIZIO
Lloyd's does, actually.

DAVE
Christ! So this is a lot more than just screwing
us for a ransom on an Old Master. What are
they after? *(reads:) è necessario rispondere
alle nostre esigenze o si perde ciò che di
valore più.* Meet our demands or you will
lose what you most value. So, what does
Venice value most dearly?

FABRIZIO

That's what you're here to help us work out,
David. You insure most of it. At the moment
we're working on two fronts. The anti-
terrorist section are certain it's an advance
warning of a full-scale terrorist attack.
I'm not convinced, yet. I'm taking a gamble,
but I think that at some point along the way,
we will get told that something very valuable
indeed will be stolen or destroyed unless we
pay up—which is precisely what happened
with the Botticelli last time we worked
together. And you stopped that happening,
without paying the ransom. That was a good
job, and I could certainly do with your help
again. *If* that's what this is, I think the
ransom demand will be made round about the
fourth or fifth target, after they've convinced
us they really mean business. So far, this is
just toying with us.

DAVE

Possibly. Nothing actually very valuable has
been attacked yet, so we have to track them
down before it reaches the really serious stage
of the game—we don't want them trashing a
Carpaccio just to show they mean it. A lot
depends on what the next one turns out to be:
potenza lascia. Something to do with boats?
—But so far, I agree, the whole thing doesn't
feel like a terrorist attack to me—you
certainly don't get seven warnings of a
terrorist attack. Any other clues? What about
those biblical references at the bottom. I'm
not a bible man so you'll have to remind me—

FABRIZIO
Well, I looked them up. I assumed they were
signatures, in some sense. But I'm baffled.
The Matthew passage is Christ walking on the
water and Peter says to him, Lord, if it's you,
tell me to come to you on the water. The Luke
verse is the thief on the cross, saying if you're
the Christ, save yourself and save us. John 1:
25 is the question to John the Baptist: why are
you baptizing if you're not the messiah or
Elijah or one of the prophets. And the
Genesis reference is Abraham to Lot, saying
go away from me: and if you go to the right, I
will go to the left; if you go to the left, I will
go to the right. Well, the only thing they have
in common is some sort of hypothetical—if
you are, if you go, and so on. But they may be
just teasing us —Matthew, Luke, John as just
the signatures on the letter, but —

*Dave's mobile phone rings. He gestures to Fabrizio
and then answers it.*

DAVE
Ah, hello. Is that Kate? —What a nice
surprise. *(pause)* Yes, I'd love to. Of course
I'm free. Absolutely. Say, forty minutes.
(pause) Yes. The garden is at the back of the
palazzo. From the vaporetto, just walk
through from the landing stage, or if you're
walking anyway come in from the side. It's,
er— turn right out of the Campo San
Barnabo, along Fonde Rezzonico and there's a
gate on your left. I'll see you there. Soon.
Glad you rang.

FABRIZIO
(grins at him) Pleasure with business, eh.

DAVE
Frankly, I didn't think this burning adverts
thing would be a big deal. Thought I'd just be
able to enjoy a few days in lovely Venice.
So —did you get that name for me?
I know I shouldn't have asked—
but you haven't seen her.

FABRIZIO
OK, David. Yes. I owe you, after all.
Her name's Yekaterina, surname Coleman.
Dual nationality, English-Russian—note the
Russian first name. But she's not staying at
the Calcina. She's at the Albergo next door.

DAVE
Interesting. Bit odd. Cheaper, maybe.
Any rate, I now have a date, for lunch.
Look, I'm going to have to think all this over.
Usual rules? I'm not officially here or part of
your investigation team, but you'll keep me
posted if you can? And I can take a copy of
the threat letter, yes. Anything else? What
about the remaining two targets?

FABRIZIO
'*più bella illusione ottica*' and '*insensato*'.
The most beautiful optical illusion. And:
insensato: senseless, meaningless. Your
guesses would be as bad as mine. But the
third one, the arches, may happen today—
it's been one target a day, so far. The
department of works has men checking all the

main bridges, looking for explosives,
anything suspicious. But so far the attacks
have been pretty mild stuff, a few small
fires—if it's a ransom pattern, I really can't
think they'd actually blow up a bridge at this
stage. But we don't know. Just be careful on
bridges today!

         DAVE
We definitely don't insure bridges.
OK, I'll think about the general pattern
—after lunch! Be in touch.

        FABRIZIO
Another thing, old friend. Your lunch date
—I did some checking. She's a freelance
journalist.

        DAVE
Is she indeed? She didn't say. Interesting.

13. EXT. ABOARD A VAPORETTO.

*Dave is aboard a vaporetto on the Grand Canal at
Salute, heading towards Rialto. Scores of people pile
on board. Some dump luggage and bags onto the
baggage rack. Others scramble to the sides to get a
good view. Most are taking photographs.
As it goes under the Accademia bridge, Dave looks
warily up at the underside of the bridge.
At Ca' Rezzonico, he gets off and pushes through the
crowd into the Casa. In the little cafe, he buys a
baguette and a coffee and then goes through to the
garden.*

14. EXT. CA' REZZONICO. GARDEN.

Kate is seated, waiting, with a baguette and a bottle of water. He comes over and sits beside her.

              DAVE
Kate, hello. You took my advice, then.

              KATE
Yes, indeed. Hello. And I hope you don't
mind if I need some more advice too.
I'm a bit bewildered by Venice.

              DAVE
Not the only one. So, where did you get to
this morning?

              KATE
I just wandered, walking, taking the
vaporettos, enjoying the water and the light,
and the buildings. It's fantastic, but all a bit
overwhelming. I do love this little garden,
though, and I thought if you can get this so
right, maybe I should pick your brains a bit
more. What would you recommend then?

              DAVE
How long have you got?

              KATE
I'm booked in till Sunday.

              DAVE
At the Calcina?

KATE

Er, sort of. I got a special deal. Last minute.

DAVE

So what do you do? And how come you've never been to Venice before?

KATE

Oh, I do this and that. I used to write a bit. About avant-garde art movements. But I'm not really into Venetian art at all, not my period, not my taste, and there's been precious little avant-garde about the place for a long while. So I never thought Venice itself was really my scene, and friends had put me off— the crowds, the tourist thing. It is pretty packed, isn't it.

DAVE

You haven't even come for the Biennale? *(slight pause)* Well, I told you, the best time to see Venice is when the tourists —that is, the other tourists—have all gone. Most come thinking they'll be sitting on their wonderful balcony overlooking the Grand Canal. They end up in some grotty hotel on the mainland, in Mestre, and have to take the train in every morning and then make sure they catch the last one out at night. The last vaporetto back to the railway station at night is sheer hell. And of course most of the people who actually work here also live in Mestre — since they can't afford the property prices, which are spiralling ever upwards thanks to the rich shits who buy an apartment for some ludicrous price and then visit it for just a few

days in the year. So the cooks, the waiters, the
gondolieri, even the policemen, all head back
to Mestre around 10.30, which is why you
can't get a meal late and the place goes dead.
Which is when I love it.

     KATE
So while I'm waiting for the last train and the
last of the other tourists to have left, where do
I go in the daylight? Where do I find the real
Venice?

     DAVE
Well, don't join the queue for San Marco, for
a start. That will really put you off, for life.
Or the Ducal Palace, unless you get up very
early. Look, if you're going to be here on
Sunday morning, I'll take you to Mass—

     KATE
(interrupts with a laugh) That's the weirdest
offer I've had for a while!

     DAVE
—to Mass in San Marco. It's by far the best
way to see the basilica—and to hear it.
Fantastic choir. You have to sit through High
Mass, in Latin. But that's fabulous in its own
way. And infinitely better than fighting your
way through a crowd of tour groups being
shepherded through the place.

     KATE
OK, that's a deal. But where do people go
who aren't tourists. I love the feel of the actual

city, the architecture, the buildings, the light,
the water. That's what interests me. I'm not,
as I said, all that keen on the kind of art they
have in the museums and galleries here.

                DAVE
But that's definitely not the way to see the art.
The best gallery in Venice is the Chorus Pass.

                KATE
The what?

                DAVE
You can buy an entrance pass, called the
Chorus, to fifteen churches around Venice,
with some absolutely marvellous paintings
and sculptures, altarpieces, frescoes, ceilings,
all *in situ*. Works by Tintoretto, Rubens,
Titian, Veronese, and lots of 'minor' artists,
but in the churches they actually produced
them for, still in place—and *that*'s when you
see what they were all about. Look, I'll take
you to see the Tintorettos in his own local
church, in the parish he barely left for the
whole of his life. He was their local painter
and decorator, not some detached artist
making works of art for gallery walls or for
wealthy connoisseurs to stand in front of with
a catalogue and an appreciative expression on
their face. Or you can see his other line of
work in the Scuola Grande di San Rocco,
where he painted enormous walls and ceilings
for the confraternity of Saint, well, Rock—

15. EXT. ON A VAPORETTO.

A vaporetto is passing under the Rialto bridge.
As it does so, suddenly thick black smoke starts to
pour out of one of the bags on the baggage rack.
There is a loud ticking noise coming from the bag.
The passengers start to panic. One of the crew lunges
towards the bag and hurls it over the side of the boat
into the water. It sinks. As panic subsides,
some cheering and clapping for the crewman.

16. EXT. CA' REZONNICO. GARDEN

Dave has clearly just finished an enthusiastic eulogy
on Tintoretto and others.

        KATE
Wow! And I thought you were in insurance,
not art history.

        DAVE
Fair point. But insurance isn't always boring,
you know. We actually insure some of those
galleries, and a lot of the paintings.
So I *have* to know about them.

        KATE
(teasing) Is that why you're here now? Trying
to sell insurance policies on Old Masters?
Special introductory offer: three for the price
of two?

        DAVE
Ah, no professional questions please.
Trade secrets. Now, what precisely
is it you do? You write —what—?

His mobile phone rings. He answers it immediately.

Fabrizio?— *(listens, longish pause)* OK.
You're heading there yourself? Where shall
we meet? —Caffe del Doge. Near enough.
Fine. Are the vaporetti suspended? No?
Then give me, say, twelve minutes. *(to Kate)*
Sorry, Kate, something's come up. Tintorettos
some other time. Er, how about dinner this
evening?

    KATE
Not this evening, no.

    DAVE
You're booked for something?

    KATE
(slightly hesitant) There's a mid-week match.

    DAVE *(incredulous)*
What? Football? You cannot be serious.
Venezia are crap! Who are they playing?

    KATE
Inter, I hope. I'm a football fan. *(grins)*
I'm from Liverpool, after all.

    DAVE *(getting up to go)*
Crazy. They're not even in Serie A, are they?
Right, tomorrow evening? How about the
Locanda Montin, at 7 pm. I'll pick you up at
6.45. That suit? But you'd better give me the
name of your hotel. *(He realises he's just
blundered.)* Or I can meet you at the Zattere
landing stage. Is that OK?

KATE
(has noticed the slip)
I'll be at the Zattere. 6.45. Fine.

17. INT. CAFFE DEL DOGE.

Fabrizio and Dave are talking over coffee.

DAVE
Well, we know they really do mean it now.
But what is it they mean? Still no specific
demands?   What's the eventual target and
what's the price? When are they going to let
us know? Another letter in the lion's mouth?

FABRIZIO
They could repeat this stunt of course, with
variations—they know we can't search every
bag every time anyone gets on a vaporetto,
and we can't realistically stop people getting
on board with their bags—but the next one
could contain explosives—and they know
that we know that. It's getting serious.

DAVE
But you think this one actually didn't contain
explosives? It was just a smoke bomb and a
loud clock? Pretty neat anyway—radio
controlled, or just a mobile phone call as the
trigger—pity they threw it into the water. But
they probably banked on that. A water-logged
burnt-out bag won't tell us much. And
salvaging it would raise too many alarms,
that it wasn't just an accident.

                    FABRIZIO
Rumours are already circulating—and there's
already footage of the vaporetto fire up on
YouTube. Venice is getting popular on
YouTube.

                    DAVE
Interesting. That was pretty fast. Who's put it
up there? That might be worth chasing?

                    FABRIZIO
We've already checked. In fact, there's quite a
few uploaders—mainly American tourists,
and a couple of local kids who were on board,
hardly suspects.

                    DAVE
You've compiled all the footage?

                    FABRIZIO
We only have what was uploaded—just a few
seconds, and of course only shows the actual
incident. Not who put the bag there in the first
place—probably way back, at Ferrovia, where
you'd expect people with luggage. Then they
got off somewhere in between, if it was fired
remotely—so we'd have to call for every
mobile phone and tourist camera on the boat
to be examined— and that's just not possible.
And it might spread real panic anyway.

                    DAVE
You're going to have to start anticipating a bit
better— if it's a ransom on, say, a church,
they've already shown they can pull
something like that off.

FABRIZIO
And now they don't even have to specify in
advance which painting or which building is
the target. If they do, we could organise some
protection, a defence. But if the message is
just 'a Rubens' or 'a church', we couldn't risk
the gamble. We'd have to pay up. Agreed?

DAVE
Sounds right. Always a lot easier than
actually stealing something and being paid to
give it back. They know they can't sell, say, a
Giorgione or a Titian anyway. This way they
don't need to..

FABRIZIO
And assessing the risk is partly up to you—
it's probably going to be your insurance at
stake, since only a Lloyd's syndicate is likely
to be involved—everbody else has pulled out
of the market after the last few ransom
attempts. At some point *you* will have to
decide how much you're willing to pay.

DAVE
There's too many targets, aren't there.
Bloody nightmare. What's the next warning?
—I'm still puzzled why have they've given us
so many? We only needed two or three at
most—we're already pretty well convinced
that they know what they're doing. They
could have stopped here. But still no
demands? Maybe we missed the post.

FABRIZIO

The next warning is the one about 'power
gives way to sail'. That could mean the target
is a cruise liner. All the cruise companies
have been told to be extra alert.

DAVE

A cruise liner? Something *really* big—
because they don't want any hesitation when
they do give us the final target? They take out
a cruise liner and then threaten San Marco
itself. What's the price of that?

FABRIZIO

What Venice most values, eh?

DAVE

Does your anti-terrorism squad still think it's
terrorism? Political? Ideological? But if so,
what's the demand, the motive, the aim?

FABRIZIO

The top brass don't buy my ransom warning
theory. They're convinced we've just been
lucky : two *failed* attempts to set fire to
things, and this last one was definitely a bomb
that also failed to go off properly. I think
those 'failures' were deliberate, but I'm in a
minority —the anti-terrorism squad are now
planning pre-emptive strikes. Known
suspects. Anarchists. Politicos. Different kind
of insurance, I suppose.

They sit sipping coffee, stumped. Pause.

                    DAVE
Something else is mildly bothering me,
Fabrizio. Different topic, I'm afraid. You say
Katerina Coleman is some kind of journalist.
What's her field? Sport?

                    FABRIZIO
Well, Google her. She does freelance features.
Modern artists, art movements. Something
like that. Didn't really register with me.

                    DAVE
Yes, that's sort of what she said herself.
But she's never been to the Biennale. Odd.
I'm just curious. A sort of hunch, maybe.
Why did she rise to my lunch bait? Flattering,
but a bit unexpected. *(pause)* OK, I'm
heading back to the Hotel Leonardo.
On the pattern we've seen so far, you've got
till tomorrow to crack the problem of power
giving way to sail—but I'm beginning to
suspect, or hope, that maybe none of this is
really my problem—that it's not an insurance
scam at all. If it's straight terrorism, we don't
pay out.. Ring me if —

18. EXT. STREET IN SANT ELENA.
AFTERNOON. SIESTA TIME.

*Several heavily armed police raid an apartment in a
working class street in the district of Saint Elena.
Three young men, perhaps Arabs, are arrested and
taken away.*

19. EXT. STREET IN SANT ELENA.
LATE AFTERNOON.

*Kate is strolling around. Long distance shots:
she stops and chats briefly to anyone she passes.
Inaudible conversations.*

20. INT. HOTEL LEONARDO ROOM.

*Dave is working on his laptop, muttering inaudibly to
himself.*

21. EXT. OUTSIDE VENEZIA FOOTBALL
GROUND. EVENING.

*Kate walks towards the the ground, hesitates.
Approaches a policeman on duty near the ground.*

> KATE
> Scusi, per favor. Da quale parte dello stadio
> per i sostenitori di Venezia?
> *(Which part of the ground for the Venice
> supporters?)*

> POLICEMAN
> Sei una tifosa dei Lagunari?! Di dove sei?

> KATE *(smiles)*
> Non, non è un fan di Venezia. Ma voglio
> osservare il calcio. E sono da Liverpool.

> POLICEMAN
> Liverpool! Liverpool! ?

> KATE *(laughs)*
> Ma non. Everton! Everton!

                    POLICEMAN
Ah, blu, non rossi! Benvenuti, signorina.
Vai alla parte a destra.

                    KATE
Grazie, grazie.

*She buys a ticket and goes to the stand with the local
Venice supporters. In a long shot, she starts chatting
to some youngsters on the terrace waiting for the
game to start.*

                    POLICEMAN
*(points her out to incoming supporters as they
pass— whispers conspiratorially:)*
La signora è da Liverpool—una scout per
l'Everton, mi creda.

WRITTEN:] Day Three: Thursday

22. EXT. STREET. DAWN.

*A police raid on another apartment block in a
different street in the Sant Elena district.
Four men, middle-aged, working class,
are bundled away in a police launch.*

23. INT. HOTEL ROOM. MORNING.

*Kate is working at her computer. Pauses. Thinks.
Makes a phone call on her mobile.*

                    KATE
Sarah?   Morning, love. You OK? *(pause)*
Yes, still in Venice. Got a moment? *(pause)*

Fine, fine. It's working out. But I need to
check some details I can't track down here.
Following a lead. There was a piece I
remember that got spiked, so it's not on-line.
About a sting operation on a paedophile
priest. *(pause)* Yes, in Venice. Three years
ago, maybe. Do a search on 'Dominic Savio',
if that helps. *(pause)* Yup. Email me anything
you can dig up. I need names. Thanks, love.
Bye.

24. INT. HOTEL LEONARDO ROOM.

Dave is reading on-line a manual of regulations.

DAVE *(to himself)*
Right: international-regulations-for-
preventing-collisions-at-sea. How boring.
But let's see what we can find.

25. INT. OFFICE.

*Fabrizio is standing looking at the very large scale
wall map of Venice. He looks frustrated and
impatient. He looks at his watch.*

26. INT. HOTEL LEONARDO ROOM.
AFTERNOON.

Dave is lying on his bed, reading a Bible, in Italian.

27. INT. OFFICE. LATE AFTERNOON.

Fabrizio is sitting at his desk, head down, fast asleep on his arms. His phone rings.

                    FABRIZIO
            (answers phone a bit groggily)
David. Hello. No, nothing to report.
(listens, laughs) You've spent the whole day
reading the Bible? In Italian? Well, it's good
for your Italian. But you've drawn a blank.
(pause) Yes, me too. OK, go to your dinner
date. Hope you have better luck. *(suddenly
remembers)* Oh yes, there is something to
report. Something a bit strange. I was going to
ring you but it seemed maybe just some sort
of a weird coincidence. Odd though.
We raided a couple of places early today,
precautions, anticipations. Nothing turned up.
But I notice from the arrest reports that one of
the men we detained had your lady's first
name and a mobile phone number on a piece
of paper. Katerina. That's not a common name
around here, after all. *(longish pause)* Yes,
well he apparently said it was just a woman
he met at the football match last night. So
nobody's done anything about it, yet. *(longish
pause)* She did, did she? Well, perhaps we
should pull her in for questioning. Or maybe
you can find out what she's up to. It looks as
if she may not be interested in you for your
good looks and charm, after all. *Ciao*!

28. EXT. FONDAMENTE ZATTERE. EARLY EVENING.

Dave and Kate are strolling along the fondamente. Coming towards them in the Giudecca Canal is a large yacht which cruises down the canal every evening, with its several masts outlined in bright lights. People are watching it from the fondamente as the sun starts to set behind it.

Suddenly a small rubber dinghy with an outboard motor rapidly comes across the water from the Isola di Giudecca. It is difficult to make out but there is a figure crouched in the stern. The dinghy is about to pass dangerously close in front of the yacht, which is hooting its horn by now, when the dinghy swerves directly into the bows of the yacht and is ploughed under the water by it, almost sliced in two. The dinghy explodes like a burst balloon. The figure in the stern disappears into the waves. Horror and consternation from those watching. A policeman on the quay starts running towards the scene, speaking into his radio.

> KATE
> *(turning away, into Dave's arms)*
> That's dreadful!

> DAVE
> *(comforts her, then very slowly:)* It *may* not be quite what you think. Just a moment, Kate.

Dave pulls out his mobile phone and makes a call, over her shoulder. She is taken aback at what seems a callous gesture. Disengages herself quickly.

                    DAVE
Fabrizio. I think I've just solved target three
for you. You'll get reports pronto.
One of your uniform guys is already on the
job. But don't believe any first reports.
I happened to be there, or rather here, on the
spot. When you can, you might join us—
at the Locanda Montin. OK?

                    KATE
You're not really an insurance salesman,
are you?

                    DAVE
I never said I was. I'm an insurance
investigator—as I think you know already,
Kate. Since you're an investigative journalist,
yes? So let's have some dinner after all—
and talk about what we're both investigating

29. EXT. GARDEN RESTAURANT AT LOCANDA MONTIN.

Dave and Kate are at a table, having a glass of wine, waiting for their order. Which duly arrives during the following exchange. They eat while talking:

                    DAVE
Right, first things first. I don't think what we
just saw was a death, or an accident.
I think the figure in the boat was a dummy
and the dinghy was radio-controlled. Nor was
it trying to blow up the yacht, which is what
the anti-terrorist squad are probably about to
proclaim to the world.

KATE

Well, that makes me feel a lot better.
But even more puzzled. What is going on,
Dave, and what's your involvement?

DAVE

You first, I think, Kate. You'd better know
that the *police* are wondering what *your*
involvement is, and in particular why your
name and phone number were on a guy they
picked up this morning in a sweep of political
activists. Yes—I have a contact in the police
—whom you'll probably meet pretty shortly.
So you'll need answers for him. Why not
rehearse them with me first?

KATE

(thinks a moment) The name and phone
number bit is quite simple. I went to the
football match last night as the easiest way to
ask a few questions to people who might
know some answers. It's wonderful how
watching a match together loosens people's
tongues. They thought at first I was a scout
for a Liverpool football club, which helped a
lot! I told them I was actually a journalist
doing a piece on how local people in Venice
have a tough time of it, by contrast with all
the well-off tourists who crowd the place out.
The Venice the tourists never see, that kind of
line. So I gave my contact details to several
people there, who said they might be willing
to talk to me about it. The guy who got
picked up was presumably one of them. Do
you know his name?

DAVE

No. But that's not *really* what you're writing
about, is it. What were those questions, Kate?
What are you really working on?

KATE

(pause) OK, I'll come clean. I've been
researching a major feature article, maybe
even a book, on some of the new protest and
resistance movements across Europe, the New
Provos in Amsterdam, the Black Cats in
Athens, the United Leprechauns in Dublin —

DAVE

(laughs) The what!

KATE *(smiles)*

Yes, United Leprechauns. Radical Greens.
Part of the point is that these new movements
use different weapons from the old ones,
including humour and comedy, and political
piss-taking. The United Leprechauns are a
hoot, and pretty effective at taking the piss out
of the established political parties and
ideologies. Any rate, I was interviewing
some French activists recently and they said
they were getting rumours on the networks of
something big about to happen in Venice, of
all places. I started to check it out, and
discovered a few websites that interested me,
something different, a new tactic. Then one
of the French guys emailed me on Monday
with the footage of those adverts going up in
flames and his message was: It's starting. So I
got the next flight here and have been trying
to dig a bit.

DAVE
Any results?

KATE
Wait a moment. It's your turn now. Your
profile's on the net if you know where to look,
so I do know you work for Lloyd's, and I
guess you're here because Lloyd's is liable for
some of the 'targets'—that was the word you
used on the phone to—was it Fabrizio?—your
police contact.

DAVE
Sharp hearing. Yes, all true. But I'm not sure
we're talking about the same thing. We,
Fabrizio and I at least, think what's probably
happening is one of those scams where the
final target is not actually damaged, stolen,
whatever. Normally it's a painting or
sculpture, which is easier to damage than to
steal, but sometimes it can be a whole
building. It's a variation on a protection
racket or a ransom demand: you make it clear
that you *could* damage something in a pretty
big way and then demand enough to stop you
from actually doing it. In some circumstances
we will pay up rather than risk losing a
Michaelangelo, a Picasso, or a Palladian villa.
Even on one occasion a super-star footballer.
They threatened to blind him. My job is to try
to put a spoke in the works *before* we reach
the endgame.

KATE
So what's the final target?

DAVE

Good question. But no answer, yet.
We don't know. Just a message: 'meet our
demands or lose the thing Venice values
most' —whatever that is—and we've had no
demands at all, yet. Only a series of pretty
low-key but worryingly competent warnings.
The burning adverts were the first, the toilets
the next, a sort of fake attack on the Rialto
bridge, and now this—whatever it was. But I
certainly don't think it was a suicide bomber.
It just doesn't fit. That was definitely only a
dummy figure in the dinghy and the collision
was deliberate, radio-controlled from a good
distance away. But why? A dummy run?
Just to show us what they could do it if they
wanted? But they've already shown us that.

KATE

Any actual clues to go on?

DAVE

Sorry, I obviously can't bring you in on
anything specific unless Fabrizio says it's OK.
He'll be here soon. *(pause)* Well, maybe there
is something you can have a crack at. It's sort
of in the public domain after all, well, in the
Bible anyway. I'm baffled. A message they
sent was sort of signed, with four names, but
the names are biblical: Matthew, Luke, John,
no Mark but just Genesis, each of them with a
verse reference. Can't remember the passages
exactly, but one was Peter asking Jesus to let
him walk on water, another was about John
the Baptist baptising, then the bad thief
mocking Christ for not saving himself, and a

weird verse from Genesis about me walking
on the left if you walk on the right and vice
versa. Baffling. I spent the day reading the
bloody Bible. In Italian!

    KATE
Do they correlate with the targets—water
with water maybe? Fire with—no, doesn't
work. Or are they paintings in the Accademia
or one of the churches—Christ walking on
water, the bad thief, and so on.

    DAVE
Good try. Interesting. There are some
paintings that would fit. That *might* be it —
but I can't find any connection with what's
happened so far, so perhaps they're not
'signatures' at all but the actual targets.
That's worrying.

    KATE
Let me think. *(drinks more wine)*
Do the passages have anything in common?
The same words? A phrase?

    DAVE
Yes, but it doesn't seem to help. Each passage
does have the same phrase: 'if you'—if you
are the Christ, if you aren't Elijah, if you
walk, etc — in Italian, *'sei si'*. If you—what?

    KATE
This is clearly a three glass problem, Watson.
More wine, I think. *(Drinks slowly. Pause.)*
Got it! And it tells us quite a lot.

Whoever wrote your message reads his, or
her, bible in Latin, the Vulgate, not in Italian.
The phrase 'if you' isn't 'sei si'— in the Latin
Vulgate, it's—I'll bet you—'si tu'.
Which means—?

                DAVE
If you—ah, in Italian 'si tu ' would be: 'Yes,
you! ' But— so what? I'm still no wiser.

                KATE
'Situ' is actually short for Situationist.
The Situs were followers of the Situationist
International. Those texts are telling you that
you're dealing with situationists. And ones
who read Latin! That should narrow the field!

                DAVE
Situationists? What the hell are they?
Hang on. Rings a pretty faint bell.
Way back in the nineteen-sixties? Paris May
events and all that?

                KATE
It fits—

*Fabrizio enters the garden, motions to a waiter to
bring some wine, and joins them, overhearing.*

                FABRIZIO
What fits?

                DAVE
Kate, meet Fabrizio. Fabrizio, Kate. Details
later. I think we can trust her, Fabrizio. OK?

Cautious greetings between Fabrizio and Kate.

                    DAVE
She might have just given us a lead.
What do you know about the Situationists?

                    FABRIZIO
Situationists? Long time ago. They were the
bunch who constantly expelled each other—
until there were only two left and one of *them*
was in a lunatic asylum, right?

                    KATE *(smiles)*
That's part of the story, yes. But at their height
they were brilliant. Provocateurs, theorists,
activists. They created the whole *style* of May
1968. They saw modern society as dominated
by the spectacle, by the media, by the
fetishism of commodities, by consumerism,
above all by the image. Guy Debord wrote a
stunning treatise, *The Society of the Spectacle*,
which spelt out their analysis, and in practice
they set out to destroy the grip of the
spectacle by creating situations, events,
happenings, which would shatter the image,
puncture the consensus, turn the media on
itself. The '68 *evenéments* for them were one
huge situation, against the spectacle. *(pause)*
And I think your guys are new situationists.

                    FABRIZIO
Well, there *were* some Italian Situationists,
but they're all long dead and gone and I doubt
if anybody's ever heard of them in Venice!
There was a guy called Sanguinetti, wasn't
there, who wrote a crazy book?

KATE

Yes, the *Rapporto Veridico*, 'on the last
chance to save capitalism in Italy'— which
bamboozled the whole ruling class in Italy
into thinking he had provided them with a
perfect stratgy for reinstating fascism—only
for him to use their responses to unmask the
secret connections between them all.
Sanguinetti sent the book anonymously to
every leading businessman, banker, politician,
media mogul, and then sat back and watched
them entangle themselves in a conspiracy
which *he* was directing. A kind of infiltration
by the left.

FABRIZIO

Well, maybe. Let me think. *(pause)*
Yes, I can see how some of what's been
happening might be Situationist in spirit—
burning those adverts, certainly.

KATE

Yup. Setting fire to a toilet!

DAVE

All the public toilets, Kate. That same night.
And then setting off smoke bombs on a
vaporetto, not a real bomb. And crashing a
fake suicide bomber into a showpiece yacht?
Are these the kind of things your situationists
would do?

KATE

Yes. Indeed. Their style entirely!

                    DAVE
But what's the point!! These are just, well,
silly jokes! Pranks.

                    FABRIZIO
Or are they just *imitating* Situationist games,
while actually plotting something far more
serious? I wouldn't get carried away by this
idea. There may still be a real sting in the tail.

                    KATE
Have they specified any more targets?

                    DAVE
Can I show her the letter? She might spot
something we haven't.

                    FABRIZIO
Wait a moment. I need to ask you something
first, Kate. What's your connection with our
local politicos, and what are you really up to
yourself? I have to warn you that we seem to
have found a connection between yourself
and a leading local trades unionist. Care to
comment?

                    DAVE
Sorry, Fabrizio, I've already told her about
the name and phone number.

Fabrizio is about to react angrily.

                    DAVE
Well, Kate? You ducked my question earlier.

KATE *(to Fabrizio)*
I've already explained to Dave that I'm
writing a piece on the new resistance
movements round Europe, and I was
following a kind of tip-off that something was
about to break in Venice. I actually had a
hunch that some version of the Situs might be
involved, because of the YouTube footage of
those huge adverts going down in flames—
which is frankly why I got the verbal clue
about 'si tu' quite so easily. Well, last night I
was trying to track down a website I thought
might be connected. One which seemed to
come right out of the kind of disaffected,
pissed-off, radicalised youth opposition
groups that are all over Europe now.
So I asked around at the football match and
gave my name and number to people who
were quite prepared to tell me where the
drugs were being dealt, where the street gangs
were operating, where the squatters were—
but nobody knew anything about the actual
website I was interested in. I'd managed to
establish that it was run from a location
somewhere in Sant' Elena and I was nosing
around to see if I could get some clues as to
who might be responsible. Is that enough?
What was the name of this connection I'm
supposed to have? Was it Antonio Rossellini?
He seemed the most genned up? Is he a
politico? Some kind of police suspect?
I obviously didn't know that.

DAVE *(tries to lighten things)*
So you weren't just trying to pick up Italian
men?

KATE *(grim smile)*
They don't need any encouragement.

FABRIZIO *(still annoyed)*
So what is this website you mentioned?
Politics? Anarchism? Situationists?

KATE
No. Not directly. And that's what's
interesting about it. It's basically just some
looped video footage and several live
webcams. But it's devastating. Because it
shows Venice as a *totally awful place to
visit*—one of the webcams continuously
shows only the most absolutely crowded parts
of the main tourist trail, another shows the
Mestre railway station, and there's repeated
footage of the last vaporettos absolutely
packed with crushed tourists trying to get to
the last train, and so on. It's a kind of *anti*
Tourist Office for Venice. And it has a
slogan: "The tourist comes to Venice hoping
for paradise and ends up eating tomato sauce
on a cold pizza." It would really put you off
coming at all!

FABRIZIO *(calming down)*
And so you think the same people are
responsible for the website and for these—
pranks? Why?

DAVE
Read her the letter, Fabrizio— the last lines.

FABRIZIO
(pulls a copy out of his pocket and reads:) —
è necessario rispondere alle nostre esigenze o
si perde ciò che più valore—

DAVE
'Or lose what Venice most values'—tourists!!
That's what their final target is. To rid the
whole place of tourists!

FABRIZIO
(pause) You're right. *(pause)* I'm afraid.
That's a pretty big target. And pretty
vulnerable —to straight terrorism.

DAVE
I can see that. But how do you get rid of
tourists? What would do that? A maniac
with a machine gun in San Marco square?
A bomb in the basilica? Or flying a plane
into the campanile? That's tomorrow's target,
isn't it?

FABRIZIO
No. Tomorrow is *'più bella illusione ottica'*
—the   most beautiful optical illusion.
The campanile is Saturday—if we're right.

KATE
Can I see the letter now?

FABRIZIO *(hesitates, then decides)*
Yes. You've given us this lead to a website.
I need the details. Write them down, Kate.
(He hands her a notebook and she does so)
And you can keep that copy of the letter.

I have lots of copies by now, all of them
scribbled over with my hopelessly wrong
guesses. *(pause)* I think you may be right, so
if you can work something out, I'd be grateful.
Maybe this *is* a sort of situationist situation.
I need to get back to the office and liaise with
the anti-terrorism squad. I'm not sure whether
this changes how they'll think about what's
happened—or is going to happen, but they're
now convinced that the episode tonight was a
real suicide bomber operation and they're
dragging the canal for the body. Of course, if
they do find a real body, your jokey Situ
notion is pretty well ruled out, isn't it?
In the meantime, Kate, all this is *strictly*
off the record, understand. *(Kates nods)*

   DAVE
OK, I'll walk Kate back to her hotel and fill
her in on anything she's still missing. We'll
ring you first thing tomorrow?

   FABRIZIO
*(calls over waiter who is anxiously trying to
close the place by now)* Sul conto della
polizia. *(to Dave and Kate:)* It's the least I can
do. Buonanotte.

30. EXT. MOONLIGHT.

*Dave and Kateare walking in wonderful moonlight.
Quietly. Then:*

   DAVE
So which hotel am I taking you to?

KATE *(bristles)*
Definitely mine.

DAVE
Sorry! No, I didn't mean that. I meant:
which hotel are you really staying at?
You told me you were at the Calcina
but you're not there, are you?

KATE
I'm at the cheaper one next door. Sorry,
but I didn't want to be pestered by some
strange man I'd met on a plane.

DAVE
Fair enough. Do I pester you?

KATE
Perhaps it's too early to say.

DAVE
Well, am I still taking you to
Mass on Sunday?

KATE *(laughs)*
If San Marco is still there — yes, please.

*They carry on walking through whatever beautiful
parts of Venice you want to enjoy here.*

WRITTEN:] Day Four : Friday

31. INT. THE FRARI CHURCH. DOORWAY.
EARLY MORNING.

*Two clerical doorkeepers are manning the door,
refusing entrance.*

*A party of four American tourists are trying to
argue their way in, led by a large loud Big Al, and all
are highly indignant.*

> BIG AL
> But we have to be at the Dogal Palace in
> thirty minutes. And I wanna see the Bellini
> first. It's in our schedule.

> DOORKEEPER
> The church is closed to tourists until 9 A.M.

An old woman in black squeezes past and goes in.

> BIG AL
> So what you letting her in for?
> The place is open, isn't it!

> DOORKEEPER
> You may come in only to attend Mass.
> Until 9 o'clock.

> BIG AL
> Right, we'll watch your mass then. That OK?

                    DOORKEEPER
(sighs, as lets them in) Please remember
this is a church, not a museum.
Please, no cameras during mass.

                    BIG AL
Jeesus, no cameras. How am I going to
remember the place? *(pulls out a plan of the
church)* Now, where's the Bellini?

                    DOORKEEPER
In the sacristy chapel. At the far side of the
church. And Mass begins there in five
minutes. Or you may attend at one of the side
chapels. Please do not —

*The group of tourists simply push past him and start
to wander, goggle-eyed. Another group appears at
the door.*

                    DOORKEEPER *(wearily)*
La chiesa è chiuso ai turisti fino alle nove.
L'église est fermée aux touristes jusqu'à neuf
heures. The church is closed to tourists. Die
Kirche ist für Touristen geschlossen.

32. INT. FRARI. SACRISTY .

*Mass is beginning at the altar of the Madonna. A
handful of worshippers.*

                    PRIEST 1 *(bows and intones)*
Introibo ad altare dei.

*Big Al takes a flash photo of the Bellini Madonna
altarpiece.*

33. INT. FRARI. TRANSEPT.

A priest in mass vestments hurries to the chapel of Bernardo, with just a small altar boy in attendance, who switches lights on in the chapel and Mass commences. No other worshippers.

34. INT. FRARI. TRANSEPT.

Another priest hurries across to the Fiorentini chapel, again with just an altar boy, who switches the lights on.

> PRIEST 2 *(bows and intones)*
> Introibo ad altare dei

He looks up at the altar— and shrieks!

> Gesù Cristo!

The altar niche is blank where the statue of John the Baptist by Donatello should be.

After a shocked pause, Priest 2 races across to the main doorway and shouts to the doorkeepers:

> Chiudere le porte. Gli allarmi! La polizia!

They quickly and strenuously close the heavy doors and activate ringing alarm bells.

As the alarms go off, the four American tourists come hurrying out of the side sacristy. As they pass the Fiorentini chapel Big Al consults his plan of the church and then looks at the empty niche above the altar.

                    BIG AL
Ah shit, I wanted to see that.

                    BIG AL'S WIFE
What's the problem dear?

                    BIG AL
Should be a nice big wooden statue of John
the Baptism. By Doonatelli Circa, 1386 to
1466. That was number two on my list in this
place. Well, that's it for here. Let's get to the
San Mark Palazzio.

They go to the door, which is firmly shut.

                    DOORKEEPER
The door is closed. Nobody leaves
until the police arrive.

                    BIG AL
The police! But we gotta leave *now*.

                    DOORKEEPER
There has been a theft. Nobody leaves.

                    BIG AL
Ah, shit! Waddyaknow. First you keep us
out, then you keep us in. That's screwed
today's schedule. Look, we're due at the cruise
ship in just three hours—

                    DOORKEEPER
      (shrugs).

35. INT. HOTEL LEONARDO ROOM.

Dave is sitting at the desk in his room, looking at a website devoted to Situationist material. He is reading Guy Debord, Society of the Spectacle, *on-line.*

His phone rings.

> DAVE
> Fabrizio? *(listens)* The Sansovino as well?
> But both are OK? I'll be there in fifteen
> minutes. Ciao.

Thinks. Makes another call.

> Kate? Sorry. Tintoretto is off for this
> morning. *(pause)* Yes, the fourth strike
> already. Ring you later. It'll probably be on
> the news anyway, but you might want to head
> for the Frari.

36. INT. FRARI.

Several police are gathered round the transept area, which has a number of police barrier ribbons stretched across it. The Donatello is back in place.

Several tourists are shepherded into a group near the door, cowed, and are being questioned.

Fabrizio is sitting quietly in a seat in the monastic choir.

37. EXT. CAMPO DEI FRARI.

Dave hurries into the square from near the Calle della Passion, and stops as he sees police barriers and a crowd near the bridge over to the Fond dei Frari. He goes over to look.

Hanging from the bridge is a life-size full colour flat cut-out figure of the Donatello John the Baptist, apparently hanging by its neck, with a note attached to its chest. Dave bursts out laughing as he reads the note. Then he strolls towards the door of the Frari.

38. INT. FRARI. CHOIR STALLS.

Dave joins Fabrizio.

>   DAVE
> I suppose it's now definitely your case, and mine, not the anti-terrorist squad after all. I like their sense of humour.

>   FABRIZIO
> You've seen John the Baptist's suicide note?

>   DAVE
> Yes: "I couldn't take it any more! Bloody tourists." *(laughs).* Show me how it was done.

>   FABRIZIO
> OK, you're officially involved now. Not sure there'll be any need for an insurance claim on this. No real damage as far as we can see. But it's now definitely your problem.

*Fabrizio walks Dave over to the Fiorentini chapel
and waves them both through the police line.*

*He reaches behind the altar and holds up a shallowly
curved sheet of stiff card, about 8 feet high and a few
feet wide, with rigid metal edging on three sides. It is
painted a grey-blue on one side, with some darker
vertical borders. Using a long pole, the kind used for
extinguishing high altar candles, Fabrizio carefully
but quickly lifts the card into position so that it slots
neatly into the front edges of the niche and clicks
firmly into place.*

*He steps back to admire the effect—which is that the
niche is now empty. An optical illusion.*

> DAVE
> Target for today: The most beautiful optical
> illusion. A leaf out of Bellini's book.
> Precisely the same trick as the Bellini
> Madonna in the sacristy, but reversed.
> Brilliant.

> FABRIZIO
> They only needed the illusion for a few
> moments and then alarms would be ringing all
> over the place before anyone spotted it wasn't
> really gone. By the time I got here they'd
> discovered the trick and taken it down.
> But the Sansovino is even better. I nearly had
> a heart attack when I saw it. We haven't
> removed it yet. Thought you'd better see if
> there's any actual damage, but I don't think
> there is.

They walk to the end of the transept and into the corner chapel, where they pause before the marble statue of John the Baptist, attributed to Sansovino. It is roped off by police ribbons. A policeman is guarding it.

The statue appears to have been attacked and badly damaged: major crack lines criss-cross the front leg and there is a deep black hole in the chest. A large iron hammer is lying on the floor beside the statue. Dave stops abruptly in total dismay.

Fabrizio waves away the policeman, and takes Dave close to the statue. He then starts to slightly peel the edge of what is now seen to be a partly transparent adhesive film, painted to give the effect of the damage, one stuck to the leg and another to the chest.

> DAVE
> Christ! I see what you mean! I was already doing frantic sums. OK, leave it now that I've seen how it was done. I'll get our sculpture experts out immediately. There may be mild surface scratches. But it doesn't look as if it'll cost us. It's just a kind of self-adhesive kitchen food wrap, isn't it. Not even any glue.

They stand looking at the statue.

> DAVE
> Helluva warning, though. *Could* have been for real. Any other surprises?

> FABRIZIO
> We've been looking. Nothing, so far.

DAVE
Let me have a wander. Worries me a bit that
the Donatello was double-pronged—the body
on the bridge as well as the optical illusion.
So is there something else going on with the
Sansovino as well?

FABRIZIO
 Nothing's missing, we're pretty sure of that.

*They wander back across the transept and into the
nave, looking around them.*

*Police, church officials and several friars are already
checking off lists at various locations around the
church.*

FABRIZIO
One clear clue: this *must* have been some
kind of inside job. The electronic eyes were
de-activated, early this morning, while the
cover was put up over the Donatello. And the
Sansovino even seems to have been done
after the first alarms were sounded—while
everybody was busy with the 'missing'
Donatello. One of the Friars swears that the
Sansovino was fine when he saw it about 7.
Pretty cool head at work. But whose? We're
still questioning the tourists who were here
but we've drawn a blank. They're either pretty
stupid or *very* good actors—and none of them
look capable of this kind of stunt. Which
leaves a few old women who have been
praying in the place for years. Or the Friars
themselves—

DAVE
—Who would hardly want this kind of
incident in their own church, especially if
there's no insurance pay-out at the end of it.
I take it this has already leaked out.
The suicidal Baptist hanging from the bridge
out there will be on the news and in all the
papers by now. So, how much can I tell Kate?
I've been reading up on her Situationists.
She might be helpful on this if we really are
dealing with a bunch of situationist lunatics.
She knows their ways of doing things better
than we do. I was supposed to meet her now.

FABRIZIO
Well, you can obviously tell her whatever's
going to make it into the press anyway.
I'm still not sure about her. But we do need to
crack the 1911 warning for, presumably,
tomorrow? She might have ideas, but this
could still be terrorism, not just teasing.

DAVE
Talking of teasing—what's that over there?

*Dave goes over to the Canova tomb, steps over the
railing, and reaches into the dark triangular
'entrance' to the tomb.*

*From it he begins to pull a large blow-up of a
postcard picture of the Sansovino Baptist, which had
been left just inside the tomb, but which is so large
that it neatly fills the cavity entrance as he tries to
pull it upright —the effect is as if it is the statue itself
which is now the focus of the mourning figures on
the mausoleum.*

DAVE *(laughs)*
Touché! I think I get the message, twice over:
Art prefers to be in the tomb rather than face
the bloody tourists! The death of the artist —
by suicide if necessary!

FABRIZIO *(is not very amused)*
Let's get that finger-printed, though I doubt if
they'd make that easy a mistake. *(motions to a
policeman to take the image)* It's not the piss-
artist that worries me. You realise that both
works are of John the Baptist, the precursor,
the one who went before —but before what?
What comes *after* this? Remember one of the
biblical texts was about John the Baptist too.
Are we right about the next target: 1911? Is it
the campanile? And is it tomorrow? I'm
getting worried again.

DAVE
I'm going to ring the London office, get
authorisation for an expert appraisal of any
damage here, explain the overall situation—
sorry, no pun intended —but talking of which,
I think I am going to have that meeting after
all with Kate, as our handy situationist expert.
(looks at his watch) Is that OK?

FABRIZIO
I suppose so. I looked into that website she
told us about. But it's using an anonymous
web-hosting service. Based in Sweden. So
tricky to get a legal handle on it. And it just
looks to me like a half-hearted schoolboy
parody of a Tourist Board website. I'm
pursuing it, but I've no real leads yet.

                    DAVE
I can tell her that, yes? *(into phone)* Kate?
Can you find the Campo San Toma—
and no need to buy a baguette on your way!
Lloyd's are paying for lunch today—
you're now a temporary consultant. OK?

39. EXT. TRATTORIA IN CAMPO S. TOMA.

*Kate and Dave are eating a light lunch at an outside
table. Dave has just been describing the morning's
events. They continue lunch during the following.*

                    KATE
OK, I get all that. The most beautiful optical
illusion was today's target. Very Situ. The
suicidal John the Baptist hanging from the
bridge was already on the news as I left.
Back in '65 or so the French Situs floated
bloodied Vietcong bodies down the Seine—
they were dummies, like the figure in the
dinghy yesterday. But I don't think they ever
used life-size postcards! What's a Situ
message for a tourist postcard: "Wish I
wasn't here"? "Wish you weren't here"?

                    DAVE
Maybe 'si tu' really does mean 'si, tu' —
'yes, *you*' — we're all tourists in Venice these
days. So, Yes, it's You who are ruining the
place. Maybe we are too.

                    KATE
Well, one thing I can suggest.
I bet they've read their Walter Benjamin.

DAVE *(munching away)*
Eh? Explain.

KATE *(enjoying her wine)*
OK, pay attention, class. Walter Benjamin,
German critic, nineteen-thirties, wrote an
influential essay on 'the work of art in the age
of mechanical reproduction'. He argued that
there had been a shift, in fact a double shift,
from the cult image, its religious aura intact,
to the art object in the museum or gallery, its
aesthetic value as the focus of a new purely
commercialised devotion—and then a further
shift to mass-produced copies, rendering the
art object cheaply accessible everywhere and
instantly at our convenience—but now
denuded of its aura. Follow that?

DAVE
(he nods, his mouth full, and a bit nonplussed)
Sort of. Go on.

KATE
Benjamin committed suicide, incidentally —
Right. So the Bellini Madonna is absolutely
the most typical cult object, in its religious
niche, its devotional aura, and at the same
time it's the most beautiful illusion, since even
the niche itself is painted so perfectly that
most people think it's a sculpture. It's flat and
two-dimensional, not three, but you can be
only a few feet away and still not realise that.
Now, play the Bellini illusion of being full-
bodied and three-dimensional off against the
Donatello being apparently stolen through the
optical illusion of not being there at all, of an

empty niche, non-dimensional— and then add
the digitally printed cut-out of it and the
touching up of the Sansovino statue —
probably done using Photoshop to get the
effects right—and you have the whole
Benjamin thesis in a nutshell. The work of art
in the age of tourism!

    DAVE
And the work of art as tourist postcard, yes?
I take it you studied art history!

    KATE
No. Much more interesting—I did a crazy
pioneering degree course called Image
Studies, not just about art but looking at the
role of all sorts of images in different
societies, different periods, different cultures
—and not just art images, but wall paintings
in Egyptian tombs, stained glass in cathedrals,
court fashions, make-up and tattoos, adverts,
cartoons, photography, film, television, digital
images— images and power, images and
women, images and identity, images and war
— you name it, we studied it.

    DAVE
Back to the point, please, Kate. Does all this
theory give us any practical clues?

    KATE
(pause) Come to think of it, Benjamin's essay
ends with a reference to images and war —
Marinetti's ' war is beautiful' — part of the
Futurist line about: 'We will glorify war—
the world's only hygiene—militarism,

patriotism, the destructive gesture of freedom-bringers, beautiful ideas worth dying for, and scorn for woman.' And so on. I remember that last bit especially, of course. Marinetti was a bloody Fascist. Benjamin's argument was that all efforts to render politics aesthetic end in war. He almost anticipates the atomic bomb in an extraordinary final passage—from memory, something like: 'This is the culmination of art for art's sake. Mankind which in the time of Homer was an object of contemplation for the Olympian gods, is now an object for its own contemplation. Its self-alienation has reached the point where it can experience its own destruction as an aesthetic pleasure of the first order.' — I always think of the end of *Doctor Strangelove* at that point. The bombs going off in a spectacular cinematic symphony. But it could also be about the kind of spectacular terrorist acts we've seen in recent years, 9/11 included. — Well, Benjamin's case is that while Fascism aestheticises politics, the Left has to politicise aesthetics. That's the kind of argument that got me interested in the Situationists in the first place—they were the logical extension of making the art-work into a political intervention—*(she realises that Dave is not listening, distracted)*—Eh, come on, David, you're not even listening — I paid attention when you talked about Tintoretto for twenty minutes yesterday!

DAVE *(thinking hard)*
Sorry, Kate. I've been trying to remember
something. You know Marinetti's infamous
'Manifesto Against Past-Loving Venice' —
all about 'filling in the small, stinking canals
with the rubble from the ancient collapsing
and leprous palaces' in order to 'prepare for
the birth of an industrial and militarized
Venice, capable of dominating the great
Adriatic, a great Italian lake' —

KATE
—Yes, of course. The one he showered all
over Venice in 20,000 pamphlets or 80,000
copies or whatever it was. He wanted to fill in
the canals and make roads for cars to take
over the city— just like some of the tourists
you meet these days. "Gee, let's turn the
Grand Canal into a fine six-lane highway—"

DAVE
Yes, yes, yes. But when was it delivered?
I'm trying to get a date right.

KATE
Well, the usual account is that he proclaimed
it through a megaphone from the clock tower
in 1910.

DAVE
From the campanile —which had been
demolished after it collapsed in 1902 and was
only fully re-opened in 1912. So the '1911'
warning might just refer to a new manifesto,
also proclaimed from the campanile, imitating
Marinetti, coming after him, as it were—

it may not refer to 9-11, the twin towers, at
all, but to Marinetti—

               KATE
What are you talking about David?

               DAVE
I'm clutching at straws. Look, you've seen the
rest of the warning letter. We're now up to
target six: which simply reads '1911'. We
assumed that it was some variation on 9-11
and that we are dealing with a terrorist attack.
But Fabrizio thought it referred not to two
towers but to the one tower built, or rebuilt,
around 1911— the San Marco campanile
itself, *the* image of Venice. I'm asking is it
going to be the target of some deadly terrorist
attack or—maybe — is it just going to be the
site for some new Situationist Manifesto?
Fluttering leaflets not charred bodies.

               KATE
Let me see the letter again.

               DAVE
I suppose so. *(gives her his copy of the letter)*
Fabrizio says the anti-terrorist section are still
taking it all very seriously, closing the
campanile for twenty-four hours, putting on
heavy security at the airport, hoping no one's
going to try to fly a plane into the campanile.
But can I really tell them it's *not* going to be
like that at all?

KATE *(shrugs)*
Better not. You may be quite wrong.
And they wouldn't listen anyway.
The precautions can't do any harm —
if it's just some sort of manifesto launch,
nothing's lost. But the Situationists were,
in their own way, deadly serious, so maybe
this really is the crunch. *(She looks at the
letter)* Look at the seventh and final warning:
Insensato—

DAVE
Literally: senseless. Maybe senseless
violence, meaningless terror. What else?

KATE
Well, it could also be a pun on incensed, very
angry. There was an English group of semi-
Situs who called themselves the Angry
Brigade. They developed out of street theatre,
a guerilla drama group. Maybe this Venice
lot are just a very angry brigade. *Incensato.*
A new Red Brigade. But their weapon, so far,
is a kind of theatre, like the tricks they played
this morning. But what are they angry about?
What are their demands? To get rid of all the
tourists? How?

DAVE
We don't really know, yet. Look, I think
tomorrow is in the hands of the anti-terrorist
squad, whatever we say. And I've cleared it
with London that we're probably not liable for
anything major — yet. I need to unwind.
So I'm going to take this afternoon off work.
Kate, finish your lunch. I promised to show

you some Tintoretto churches. Since we're
nearer the Scuola di San Rocco, let's start
there instead. Ruskin called it one of the three
indispensable buildings in Italy. And it's just
round the corner—

40. INT. INSIDE SCUOLA DI SAN ROCCO.

*The upper room. Kate and Dave are standing in the
middle. The camera tracks round the room,
observing the paintings. And the woodwork.*

> DAVE
> Ruskin says—

> KATE
> Shush. Shush. Shush.

*He lets her look in silence. Several dissolves to
indicate time passing as she wanders the room.
Finally, he takes her hand and leads her gently
towards the side room, the Salla dell'Albergo.
He leaves her in the doorway, with the enormous
Tintoretto Crucifixion facing her.*

41. EXT. OUTSIDE MADONNA DELL'ORTO.
AFTERNOON.

*Dave and Kate are in the little square outside the
church.*

> DAVE
> OK, Kate, you wouldn't let me talk in the San
> Rocco Scuola. Try stopping me here. *(smiles)*
> My favourite church in Venice. Used to be
> dedicated to St Christopher, patron saint of
> travellers and merchants —you can see his

statue over the door—and that *(points to the left side of the square)* is still the Scuola of Santo Cristofero—this was once the main entry point for merchants from the north— originally founded by a curious order of poor weavers, called the Umiliati, the lowly ones, but then taken over by a bunch of wealthy Venetian noblemen—and a usefully miracle-working statue of the virgin and child soon led to the change of name, to Madonna dell'orto— Lady of the Garden—you don't get too many gardens in Venice, mind. There's a whole social history in that shift of patrons—

      KATE
And Tintoretto?

      DAVE
Yes, this was Tintoretto's local church. Or, better, Tintoretto was a local parishioner. He lived at number 33-99, just round the corner. There's still a Casa Tintoretto. He worked for this church on-and-off for thirty years, and then his son, Domenico, followed him into the ecclesiastical painter and decorator business. Tintoretto & Son. Actually he was really called Jacopo Robusti —Jacob the Strong. Changed it to Jacob the Right Colour. Tinto Retto. Must have looked better on the van. *(she looks quizzically at him and he smiles).* I'm joking. Actually, his Dad was a *tintor* — a dyer, so he was The Little Dyer.

They enter the church.

42. INT. MADONNA DELL'ORTO. NAVE.
AFTERNOON.

*They stand in the nave. Then Kate gradually
wanders down the nave and across to the far right
wall, and stops in front of The Presentation of the
Virgin in the Temple. As she looks at it, Dave quietly
joins her and waits for a while.*

                    KATE
          Has this been damaged? There seems to be
          a line right down the middle.

                    DAVE
          Spot on. But not quite. It was originally in
          two halves. But that's because it was painted
          for the two outer doors of an organ. Which
          used to be in that space just to the right of the
          sanctuary. Ruskin, and William Morris,
          would have approved. The work of art as the
          art of everyday work. Good solid job.
          Paint an organ cover and create a masterpiece.
          In fact, several.

*Dave takes her gently by the shoulders and steers her
towards the sanctuary, stopping in front of the
paintings of St Peter and of St Paul.*

                    DAVE
          When you opened the doors to play the organ,
          on the insides of the two doors were these:
          The Beheading of Saint Paul and *The
          Apparition of the Cross to Saint Peter.*
          Nowadays, we think of them as art works, so
          too good for merely decorating an organ, so
          we put them up on the wall as if in a gallery—

KATE *(totally unimpressed)*
I'm sorry, Dave, but I was brought up a good
Liverpool Catholic —I've been trying to
respond, but all I can see are versions of those
god-awful religious pictures I knew as a kid.
They really don't *do* anything for me. I'm not
even sure I know what they're on about.

DAVE
Ah. *(long pause)* Well, you were right about
the two halves, to begin with. So go back to
the *Presentation. (They do so)* On the right of
the picture, there is glorious light and
sunshine, on the women, the children, and
above all on the little Mary, going up the
steps towards the High Priest — but on the
left, largely in shadows and even in darkness,
are the Jews—we're just by the Ghetto—the
Old Testament, the world of the Old Law—
there are a few patches of light, perhaps the
prophets who foretold the coming of the
Messiah, the Christ child, but the new
revelation, the new Temple, the New
Testament, is still to come—the true Church
of Saints Peter and Paul which we see — *et
voila!* —when the organ doors open and the
liturgy actually gets under way— *(he moves
her back to the chancel)* But now think of
when Tintoretto painted these pictures. And
for whom. The 1550s —the height of the
ferocious battle between Protestants and
Catholics — we're half way through the
Council of Trent —and the biggest battle of
the lot is over faith versus works. This isn't
just about Christians overcoming Jews, but

Rome versus Geneva —Peter and Paul were both martyred in Rome, in the papal city, beheaded and crucified—Peter of course has his keys pretty prominently with him —

        KATE
(points to a number of large keys dangling between St. Peter's legs)
Interesting place to put them too!

        DAVE *(laughs)*
Absolutely! Power and potency! You get the point. But we've suppressed that kind of reading. Nowadays, people want their art without polemics, without argument. They think it's somehow wrong for art and politics to mix. But even these 'Renaissance masterpieces' were actually polemical, theological weapons for the illiterate, fighting a battle with paint as well as words. *(pause)* Look at those two huge paintings either side of the altar area. On the left, the Golden Calf, the idol of false worship, the worship of money, of gold —this is a church for merchants after all—and on the right, that magnificent Last Judgement—where what you *do* in life will be judged. But there's no point in a Last Judgement, if like the Calvinists, you think the whole thing is predetermined, that you're predestined to either Hell or Heaven, or if like the Lutherans you think it's only faith that matters, not how you actually behave in life—now look up, above the altar—those four women are Strength, Prudence, Justice, Temperance —

the four Virtues you have to practise if you
are to lead a good life —

                KATE
I'm glad they're women, anyway! —

                DAVE
— *(still in full flow)* and just to ram home the
point about good works, we're actually
looking at one: Tintoretto did those two huge
paintings just for the price of the materials,
almost as a gift to the church. Admittedly, the
materials would have cost a helluva lot— the
paintings are each 16 meters high by 6 meters
wide — but they're not a bad advert for
someone who wanted to land the huge San
Rocco contract!

                KATE
OK, I take your point, that maybe these aren't
just the wishy-washy devotional pictures I
grew up with. If you put them into the context
of the politics and the polemics of the time,
and the sheer hard work and craftsmanship, I
can appreciate them a bit more—But I still
don't have to like them! Not my taste at all,
I'm afraid, Dave. I'm completely and utterly
unmoved. I told you I didn't respond to
Venetian art. But thanks anyway.

She shrugs and turns away.

43. TRAGHETTO LANDING STAGE.
MARCUOLA.

*They are waiting for the little traghetto to make its
way back to the landing stage.*

> DAVE
> One decent practical tip for Venice.
> Don't waste money on buying thirty minutes
> in a gondola for some ludicrous price.
> You can get the same experience, of being too
> horribly close to some pretty filthy water,
> for just one euro. Maybe one fifty. Just take a
> traghetto across the Grand Canal. Like the
> locals. Though there are only a handful of
> crossing points left these days. Er, it's normal
> to stand upright during the crossing.

*Kate looks horrified at this. But scrambles in when
the traghetto arrives.*

44. EXT. STREETS NEAR HOTEL CALCINA.
EARLY EVENING.

Kate and Dave are walking back.

> DAVE
> We're nearly at the hotel. Are you sure I can't
> take you to dinner?

> KATE
> Sorry, Dave. But remember I'm a working
> girl. I have an article to get on with. And
> various other things I have to do.

                    DAVE
In that case, just a brief detour, if I may?
Somewhere special.

                    KATE
The Guggenheim's nearby isn't it ?
More my taste.

                    DAVE
That'll be closed by now, I'm afraid.
Catch it first thing when it opens tomorrow.
No, just a little spot worth knowing about.
OK?

Kate nods. They walk.

45. EXT. THE DOGANA POINT. EVENING

*Kate and Dave sit quietly, looking across at the
expansive view towards S. Marco.*

                    DAVE
I sat on the Dogana's steps
For the gondolas cost too much, that year,
And there were not 'those girls', there was one
face—

Kate turns to look at him.

                    KATE
So who are you reciting?
Not for the first time, I suspect —

                    DAVE *(grins)*
Touché. It's Ezra Pound, the *Cantos* —

                    KATE
Bloody Fascist. Great poet though.

                    DAVE
And a great view, you have to admit.

                    KATE
Yup. Thanks for that. *(she points)*
Across the water—isn't that Vivaldi's church?

                    DAVE
Yes. How come you know that?

                    KATE
I watched a TV programme with a friend of
mine, Sarah. All about how Vivaldi wrote
music for the women's choir there, who sang
all the parts, including even the bass voices.
We decided we wanted to visit it some time.

                    DAVE *(pauses)*
Well, there may well be a concert on there
tomorrow. Do you want to go?

                    KATE
I thought everything was likely to be
cancelled tomorrow.

                    DAVE
Maybe we should just get out of the main part
of Venice altogether tomorrow?

                    KATE
I've enjoyed today.

                    DAVE

Tomorrow? Torcello, perhaps?
The island and the basilica.

                    KATE

Let's see. Ring me. I'll go to the Guggenheim
by myself, first thing. After that. Maybe.

46. INT. KATE'S HOTEL ROOM

*Kate is making a phone call, with her laptop open in
front of her.*

                    KATE

Sarah. How are you, luv? *(pause)* I've got
something nice to ask you about later. But
first, yes, I just got your email. OK, now
have you got the full story there? I need a
names reminder. I remember the basic story.
They filmed this paedophile priest more or
less in the act. Yes? And there was an
almighty row. But it never got to court.
But what was the name of the kid who set up
the sting operation? *(listens)* Yes! I was right!
Rossellini. Marcello Rossellini. And this
blog essay you said you'd found. It's by
Rossellini? *(pause)* Went on-line last year.
'On the poverty of tourist life'. Modelled on
the Strasbourg pamphlet 'On the poverty of
student life'. Yes, I'm just downloading it
now. *(she starts to read)* 'We might well
say, and no one would disagree with us, that
the tourist is the most universally despised
creature in Italy, apart from the priest and the
policeman...' Yes! *(listens to phone)*

So, what was the problem, Sarah? *(laughs)*
No, I see. Not the Doge, Domenica Selvio.
But Dominic Savio, patron saint of altar boys.
No wonder you couldn't find it for a while.
The altar boys in the paedophile sting were all
members of the Dominic Savio Guild.
(listens) Yes, I know. Domenica Selvio was
the doge who demolished the Campanile in
1080, in order to rebuilt it more safely.
(pauses) Maybe there is a connection.
 Look, luv, check the papers tomorrow.
Now, about that other thing —

47. INT. FABRIZIO'S OFFICE. MORNING.

WRITTEN:] Day Five: Saturday

FABRIZIO

(on the phone to Dave, very angry)
Have you seen the Venice papers this
morning, David. *L'Arena, Il Gazzettino,
La Nuova Venezia* — they've all got the full
story, and they've all done special editions—
they've printed the the letter, got photos, the
lot. But they're presenting it as terrorism.
Not just the Donatello incident, but all the
incidents, the adverts, the toilets, the smoke
bomb under the Rialto bridge —so somebody
must have given them inside information.
Your friend Kate is a damn journalist!—
and I gave her a copy of the letter. Including
the warnings for today and tomorrow.
Off the record! But she couldn't resist a
scoop, could she? *(pauses, listens)* Why
would she leak it to the local papers?

I don't know. But I'm now off the case completely — they think *I* leaked it and in a sense they're right, thanks to you. The anti-terrorism squad are completely in charge now. There's going to be a complete lock-down. The tourist companies are furious. And the cancellations have started— *(he slams down the phone).*

48. INT. HOTEL LEONARDO ROOM

Dave is on the phone to Kate:

                DAVE
You didn't leak it, did you, Kate? *(pauses, listens)* OK, Kate, but I had to ask. I made that point to Fabrizio but he was too angry to listen. At least I'm also now off the case— Lloyds doesn't pay out on terrorist acts. And if you're right, then the Situationists' strategy is working —apparently tourists are frantically cutting short visits and making cancellations. The papers' reports about terrorist attacks are panicking everybody. And the security measures are just making it worse. It's going to be difficult to move in the central area today. I suggest we simply get out of the main island entirely today. So how about going across the lagoon to the oldest part of the Venice archipelago, the first cathedral, at Torcello? Want to join me after all? *(pause)*

49. INT. HOTEL ROOM

Kate is on the phone:

>   KATE
> Sarah, did you check out flights? *(pause)*
> Thought so. Lots of special last minute
> offers, eh. OK, I'll book us into the Hotel
> Calcina. And I'll meet your flight on Monday.
> *(long pause)* Yes, but I really don't know
> what to do. It's not my job to turn them in.
> Have they even committed a crime?
> But I may be missing out on a good scoop—
> I'm going to have to think about this.

50. ON THE LAGOON FERRY

*Dave and Kate are standing at the rail as the waters
swish by.*

>   DAVE
> So, isn't it time you told me a bit more about
> yourself, Kate? You mentioned you were
> from Liverpool, brought up a good Catholic,
> you said, and you did some degree in Image
> Studies, was it? And you're a freelance
> journalist, yes? But that's about all I know—
>
>   KATE *(hesitates)*
> Well, there are a few more things you should
> know —
>
>   DAVE *(continues)*
> —for a start, how come you got into all this
> Situationist business? Not everybody's cup of
> tea, is it?

KATE *(slight shrug)*
Ah, that's easy. I'm named after my great-grandmother, who was Russian. Yekaterina. I never knew her—she died before I was born. But when I was doing the usual rebellion teen thing against my family, who were pretty straight-laced conservatives, even Latin Mass Society Catholics and all that *(he looks blank)*—well, I knew vaguely that she'd been swept up in the after-math of the Russian Revolution and had known all sorts of interesting people. She had been a great friend of Elsa Triolet *(he again looks blank)* — and so I ended up doing my PhD on her.

DAVE
On your great grandmother? Isn't that unusual?

KATE *(laughs)*
No. On Elsa Triolet —

DAVE
Oh. *(pause)* Who?

KATE *(getting enthusiastic)*
Elsa was born Ella Kagan, in Moscow, in 1896. In 1915 she brought the young poet Mayakovsky home to meet the family—and he promptly fell in love with her older sister, Lily, who was then marrried to Osip Brik — but the Briks believed in an open marriage, so that trio became a *ménage à trois* for several years, as well as founding *LEF,* the revolutionary critical journal —but Ella,

left in the cold, went off and married a
French cavalry officer instead and moved to
France. Hence the name Triolet. But then
Viktor Shklovsky fell in love with her—and
she allowed him to write daily letters to her
—provided he didn't mention love in them.
So that's how he wrote his great novel,
Zoo: Or Letters not about Love.
My absolutely favourite novel. Any rate,
Ella, now Elsa, divorced the French officer
and married Louis Aragon, the ex-Dadaist and
Surrealist poet. It was Elsa who recruited him
into the Communist Party. During the Nazi
Occupation they ran a Resistance cell, and
then after the war she wrote political novels
—she was the first woman to get the Prix
Goncourt —while Louis —

    DAVE
Hang on, hang on. I haven't a clue who all
these people are!

    KATE *(snorts)*
Ah. Of course. That's part of the problem
these days. You can quote Ezra Pound —

    DAVE *(grins)*
Well, only that bit, to be honest—

    KATE
— and you know about Renaissance art, and
Tintoretto, and where to get a decent lunch in
Venice— but like most people you've utterly
forgotten the great heroic periods of modern
art, of modernist art, that extraordinary
interweaving of art and politics in the 1920s,

1930s, and into the 1960s —which is when the original Situationists flourished. 'Art' now means either hushed art galleries or publicity stunts — did you see the skull as we came along the Grand Canal that first night?

                DAVE
What skull?

                KATE
Yes. Brilliant in its futile way. Outside one of the palazzi, somebody had constructed a ten-foot-high human skull—made out of crushed tin cans —a piss-take on the most expensive art work on the market this century, Damien Hirst's diamond studded skull—by the biggest earning artist ever. God help us! Any rate —

Dave's mobile phone rings and he answers it.
Listens for a while.

                DAVE
That was Fabrizio. Ringing to apologize. To you. He checked with the newspapers, and they had all received an original of the warning letter. Not the photocopy he had given us. Which is a relief. But he says that there are armed police and soldiers all around the San Marco Square. Even anti-aircraft gun emplacements. Any tourists still left are freaking out. But nothing's actually happened. Yet.

51. INSIDE BALCONY OF BELFRY OF
CHURCH OF S. BARNABA.

*Close-up of two hands holding a control panel with
a small joystick.*

52. INSIDE BALCONY OF BELFRY OF
CHURCH OF S. GIORGIO MAGGIORE.

*Close-up of two hands holding a control panel with
a small joystick.*

53. INSIDE BALCONY OF BELFRY OF CHURCH
OF S. STEFANO

*Close-up of two hands holding a control panel with
a small joystick.Hand turns to show wrist-watch. It is
a few minutes before noon.*

54. EXT. LANDING STAGE AT TORCELLO.

*Kate and Dave disembark. They begin walking along
the path towards the cathedral.*

55. EXT. HIGH AERIAL SHOT ABOVE THE
GRAND CANAL.

*Three small-scale model aircraft are flying in a V
formation along the line of the Grand Canal, high
enough easily to clear the roofs of all the buildings.*

*Camera tracks them as they fly round the great bend,
then high over the Ponte dell'Accademia, and then
past Santa Maria della Salute.*

56. INSIDE BALCONY OF BELFRY OF S.
GIORGIO MAGGIORE.

*Viewpoint from above the hand-held wireless control
box, as a hand manipulates the joystick and operates
a set of three switches.*

57. EXT. HIGH AERIAL SHOT ABOVE S.
MARCO BASIN

*Two of the model aircraft curve towards the
campanile, while the third starts to nose-dive
towards Harry's Bar on the waterfront.*

*Sudden bursts of anti-aircraft fire leave smoke-balls
near the model aircraft. Tracer bullets whine past
them. The model aircraft duck and weave.
No aircraft are hit.*

*As the two targetted at the campanile approach
nearer over the waters in front of the S. Marco
vaporetto landing stages, they suddenly explode and
fall into the water.*

*The third plane dives lower and picks up speed.
A trap opens in its fuselage and out flutter scores of
pieces of paper which flutter onto the pavement of the
Sestiere and the garden behind.*

The plane then crashes into the wall of Harry's Bar.

58. INT. INSIDE HARRY'S BAR.

*The bar is packed. The American tourist, Big Al, is
about to drink a very large Bellini, the house
champagne and peach drink.*

*As the last model plane loudly hits the roof,
Big Al splutters on his drink and spills it all down his
floral T-shirt.*

                    BIG AL
          Jesus wept! My Bellini!

59. EXT. OUTSIDE TORCELLO CATHEDRAL.
BRIGHT SUNSHINE.

*Dave and Kate are standing watching a noisy and
very lively local wedding party being endlessly
photographed by both several official and dozens of
amateur photographers in the area outside the
cathedral doorway.*

                    KATE
          Well, Dave, there is one other thing I have to
          tell you, a little late perhaps —

60. INT. TORCELLO CATHEDRAL.

*Dave and Kate are standing looking at the 12th-
century wall-high mosaic of the Last Judgement on
the west end wall.*

*The camera slowly pans across the mosaic, coming to
rest on the Lake of Fire—the souls in Hell.*

                    DAVE *(quietly)*
          You know, there wasn't much you could teach
          the church in the middle ages about the power
          of terror.

61. EXT. OUTSIDE SMALL CAFÉ ON PATH FROM TORCELLO CATHEDRAL.

Dave and Kate are sitting at one of the small tables, with a snack and a drink.

                    DAVE
          Thanks, anyway, for telling me. *(pause)*
          Have you any more surprises?

                    KATE
          Well, I do. But I'm not sure I should share it.
          (pause) Unless you absolutely promise not to
          tell Fabrizio, or anyone else.

                    DAVE
          I suspect I know what it might be. *(pause)*
          In which case, yes, I promise.

                    KATE
          I'm pretty sure who the Venice Situationists
          are. But I don't want to give them away.
          I think I'm on their side.

                    DAVE *(laughs)*
          A lot of people will be. All those tourists who
          have ever been to Venice and wished all the
          other tourists hadn't! Say no more. I don't
          want to know. Let's just get back and see
          what they've been up to today.

62. EXT. S. MARCO VAPORETTO STATION.

Dave and Kate disembark. Dave offers a handshake.

> DAVE
> I'll say goodbye here, I think, Kate.
> It's been enjoyable, while it lasted.

> KATE
> *(she declines to take his hand)*
> Are you sure, Dave? You've forgotten?
> You did promise to take me to Mass
> tomorrow. You're not going to let a girl down
> on an offer like that, now are you?

> DAVE *(laughs)*
> I hadn't forgotten! Yes, of course. I thought
> you would think I was just pestering you.

> KATE
> No. I think it's possible to be just friends—

> DAVE
> Fine. No problem. OK, then. I'll meet you at
> the *side* door to the basilica at 8.45 prompt.
> Wear a veil or something of the kind.
> Black is best!

63. EXT. AT SIDE DOOR OF SAN MARCO
BASILICA.

WRITTEN:] Day Six: Sunday

*Dave is waiting, in a suit and tie, looking anxiously
at his watch. Kate arrives in a hurry, carrying
several international newspapers.*

KATE
Didn't know if you'd seen these. I just pinched
them from the lobby of the Calcina! It's front
page on most of them.

*Kate shows him the New York Times Global Edition,
International Herald Tribune, Observer International
— headlines include 'Terrorist Threat to Venice',
'Venice Under Attack', etc.*

DAVE
We're going to have to go in — they'll be
closing the doors soon. I didn't check the
news on-line this morning. What's the gist?

KATE
They've all received a second threatening
letter — and it has a set of demands—

*They have reached the side door, guarded by
unfriendly gatekeepers.*

DAVE
Put your veil on, Kate. *(she does so)*
Messa domenica, per favore, messa della
domenica *(to gatekeepers, who suspiciously
wave them through).*

64. INT. INSIDE S. MARCO BASILICA.

*Dave and Kate enter the basilica and follow the
crowd round to the nave. They find seats near the
front of the central area of the nave. Kate looks
round and up above her in genuine amazement at the
mosaics glittering in the lights and the candles lit for
High Mass.*

DAVE *(whispers)*
Right, what are the new threats — and the
new demands?

KATE
(rustling through the newspapers)
They're basically threatening germ warfare.
Chemical and bacteriological attack. Plague
and infections. They say they will release
poisonous gases — causing food poisoning,
diarrhoea, fevers —

DAVE
They shouldn't have any problem doing that
in Venice! Just the under-cooked fish does it
quite well already.

*The mainly Italian women in the seats behind and
around them start to hush them, telling them to be
quiet, that they're in a church, and shouldn't be
reading newspapers in church —but some of them
are also listening to what Kate is saying.
And passing it on to others.*

DAVE *(whispering)*
So what are their demands?
Have they made any?

KATE *(rustles through the papers)*
There's a list. They want those huge adverts
banned, and plastic bottles banned, there are
190 million of them every year, they claim—
and they want more drinking fountains, and
more public toilets—they want cruise ships
banned from the San Marco basin—more

gardens and kids' facilities, more schools in
Venice itself—a massive tax on empty and
under-occupied properties—more ambulance
motor boats to ferry the disabled—no cars on
the Guidecca —

*The procession for the start of High Mass has now
begun, and Kate is very firmly shushed by those
around them.*

>   KATE
> *(continues, whispering very quietly)*
> And all this to be agreed and guaranteed
> before the Papal visit to Venice next month,
> or else —

>   DAVE *(whispers back)*
> OK, we'd better shut up, or we'll get lynched.
> Nothing we can do about it now anyway.
> Just enjoy the music and the spectacle.

>   KATE *(whispers, and grins)*
> Remember, I was once a Catholic —but I
> admit this is nothing like my grotty parish
> church back home! The mosaics are fabulous!

*They finally fall silent, to the continued tutting and
shaking of heads of the worshippers around them.*

*The Mass proceeds with splendid ceremony and
awesome choir music.*

65. INT. S. MARCO BASILICA.

*Several cross-fades to indicate slow passing of time
as the sung Mass proceeds. Until:*

As a normal part of the continuing ceremony, the clergy gather in the centre of the sanctuary. An altar boy comes forward with the incense bowl for the thurible to be filled. A sacristan holds out the incense bowl towards a priest, who takes a spoonful of incense and puts it onto the burning charcoal in the thurible. He adds another spoonful and closes the thurible. Then he goes towards the congregation and swings the thurible towards them to bless them.

As he does so, thick green smoke comes slowly out of the thurible and begins to fill the sanctuary. The priest starts coughing and others quickly follow suit —one of the younger altar boys starts to choke and falls to the floor—then another—and panic sets in.

The clergy struggle to escape the fumes. The priest drops the smoking thurible which continues to spew out green fumes.

The front rows of the congregation start to panic. With a great clattering of chairs, the entire alarmed congregation begins to clear the nave and side aisles, crowding towards the exits.

> DAVE *(to himself)*
> *Incensato!* Bingo!

He realises Kate is no longer sitting next to him, and spots her going towards the side of the sanctuary. He follows her and pushes through the panicking crowd just in time to reach her as she speaks across the altar rails to an older altar boy who is shepherding people out of the sanctuary.

                    KATE
          Marcello Rossellini!

*The altar boy, who is about sixteen, looks startled but
then acknowledges her.*

                    KATE *(smiles at him)*
          Si tu es Marcellus? Vel *si tu* es amicus
          scriptoris Guido Debord, et *si tu* volas ,
          bibete postea cum nobis? coffea arabica — ?

                    MARCELLO *(quickly but cautiously)*
          Si tu ? Si tu ? —Vero. Sed si tu non es
          guardia, quare mihi dicisti?

                    KATE
          Etiam legi librum admirabile et laudabile :
          Societatis Spectaculorum.

                    MARCELLO *(hesitates)*
          Comprehendo. Casa Floriana, hoc vespere,
          ad horam octodecimam.

*Kate and Dave are swept out with the rest of the
crowd.*

66. EXT. PIAZZA S. MARCO.

*Crowds are milling about, the exiting congregation
battling with the baffled tourists waiting to get in.
As word of the 'poison gas' spreads, people begin to
leave the piazza hurriedly.*

*Dave and Kate retreat towards the centre of the
piazza.*

> DAVE

So what was going on there, Kate?

> KATE

My Latin's a bit rusty, but I just made a date
with a Situationist.

> DAVE

Didn't think he was your type.

> KATE

Don't be jealous. We're meeting him for
coffee at Florian's at six this evening. OK?
So, if you'll treat me to a coffee now, I'll
explain.

67. EXT. OUTSIDE QUADRI COFFEE HOUSE. IN SAN MARCO SQUARE.

*Kate and Dave are seated at a pavement table, with
expensive coffees.*

> DAVE

Good job you're still a temporary consultant
to Lloyd's. They're paying for this.
Not sure I could afford this place *and*
Florian's in one day. Now, earn your
hideously expensive coffee.

> KATE *(sips coffee)*

But very *good* coffee. Ah, this is the life.

> DAVE

Spill the beans! Who was that?

KATE

Marcello Rossellini. He's the son of the trade
unionist official who was arrested. He was at
the match with his father, which is why I
recognised him. But I already knew who he
was.

DAVE

And that is —?

KATE

A few years ago, he set up a sting operation
on a paedophile priest. He was then a junior
altar boy in one of the Venice churches, but
not in the Basilica itself. And the altar boys
got together to catch this guy. Even had a film
of him, almost *in flagrante delicto.* Or do I
mean *flagrante dilecto?* Any rate, despite the
clear evidence, the whole thing was hushed
up. But I did write a news piece on it, which
was never published. I remembered it partly
because it just seemed so right that a boy
named Rossellini should make a film of the
actual crime!

DAVE

So is he the only Situationist?
All this, just one teenager?

KATE

No, no. But that's one of the things I want to
ask him about. All the kids involved in the
original sting will have grown up by now,
but I suspect they still know each other,
and they probably have younger brothers—
this was a team effort, I'm sure. I doubt if he'll

tell us the details, but I do want to know how
he came across the Situationists, and a few
other things like that. I'm still trying to write
that article, but I can leave out anything that
would actually give him away.

		DAVE
So we meet him this evening, and Lloyd's will
pick up the bill at Florian's. But in my report
I can't use anything you've found out?
And I can't tell Fabrizio, obviously.

		KATE
You can write your report saying you have it
on good authority that it was a situationist
intervention. But Lloyd's don't actually have
to pay out any insurance, do they? They
haven't actually damaged anything.
Well, not much.

		DAVE
I suppose not. So *(melodramatically)* my task
here is done. I shall, sadly, leave Venice.
Back to work tomorrow. *(pause)* In that case,
I shall go and see my beloved Tintorettos this
afternoon. There are lots more of them.
I can't tempt you?

		KATE *(smiles)*
No way, Dave — In any case, I have to move
out of my little albergo. Move next door, into
the Calcina, finally.

		DAVE
When does Sarah arrive?

KATE
Tomorrow. Flight 8566. Been a long week, in its way.

DAVE
Right, see you at Florian's. At six.

68. EXT. PAVEMENT TABLES IN AREA OUTSIDE FLORIAN'S.

The tuxedo orchestra is playing schmaltz music. Early evening light.

Kate, Dave and Marcello are seated at a table, with cakes, coffee, spritzers.

MARCELLO
(reasonable but hesitant English)
— so we will all find ourselves with no jobs worth having, serving the tourists, most of us not able to live here, going back to Mestre dog-tired every night, and watching our beautiful city slowly become more and more —how do you say—commercializzate—they want to build a metro, for the tourists, they want cars, they want night clubs 24 hours a day, they want adverts along the Grand Canal —so we do not want *them*—we will frighten them away!

KATE
You were the oldest? Weren't there any adults involved at all? Not even your father?

MARCELLO *(smiles)*
Papà! No, no. He is sindacalista. The old
ways.

DAVE
Then how did you pay for all this?
The rubber dinghy? The radio-controlled
planes? The website?

KATE *(smiles to Marcello)*
He's in insurance! Always the bottom line!

MARCELLO
The Vatican paid us off. When we demanded
to take that priest to the court. We used that
money. To buy giocattoli—toys —a boat,
aeromodelli. We used children's things—
catapulta, firecrackers, candelotto fumogeno,
puzza bomba —

*Fabrizio has come behind them, quietly, and has
been listening.*

FABRIZIO *(he sits at the table)*
—a smoke bomb, and a stink bomb—
Hello, Dave. Evening, Kate. Ciao Marcello.
Do I get a coffee, then?

DAVE *(startled)*
Well, yes. Erm — *(he signals to the waiter)*

FABRIZIO
It's so nice that I am not investigating any
crimes at the moment. I am free of all duties,
and I can just relax and have a coffee with my
friends. At Florian's indeed!

KATE *(wary)*
How did you, er —?

FABRIZIO *(enjoying this)*
I am a great admirer of your English detective
writer, G. K. Chesterton. His Father Brown is
very good. Do you remember the story in
which nobody saw who had done the crime?
Because nobody sees a person whom
everybody takes for granted? The postman,
for example.

*The waiter comes with coffee and Fabrizio slowly
sips it. They wait for him.*

FABRIZIO
It was the Frari that gave it away. Who is
taken for granted in a church? Who is never
seen or looked at — except perhaps for the
wrong reasons. The altar boys. It had to be the
altar boys who did the tricks in the Frari,
the Donatello, the Sansovino. *(another sip)*
And now this new letter. Threatening all sorts
of horrors before the Pope's visit next month
—but that papal visit is not yet announced,
officially. Though the boys in the San Marco
choir have already been rehearsing for it,
have they not Marcello? *(another slow sip)*
After that, it was very elementary, my dear
David. And now —

DAVE
Fabrizio, you can't. You have no proof.
And we won't help, will we Kate? As far as
Lloyd's are concerned, there is only some
minor damage to those damn adverts—

we'll fork out for them. But we'll make it a
condition that they are removed from the
buildings—and it's not a crime to blow up
your own model aeroplanes—and—

FABRIZIO
— well, there are certainly six public toilets to
be considered. *(pause)* Though they were in
pretty bad condition. They needed replacing,
I suppose. And then there's the violation of
the maritime regulations, which we have to
take most seriously, of course —*Potenza
lascia il posto a vela regola* — and then —
but most luckily, none of these crimes are in
my department. No, there is just one small
matter that puzzles me in all this. I merely
wanted to ask Marcello a question, as one
Venetian to another . I am a true Venetian,
after all, David and Kate.

MARCELLO *(suspiciously)*
You have not said who you are.
Though I can guess. What is your question?

FABRIZIO
Thank you, Marcello. *(pause)* Now, it seems
that you met Kate here at the football match,
when you went with your father. So my only
question, Marcello, as one true Venetian to
another, is: why on earth do you go and watch
Venezia! They're terrible!

*They all burst out laughing. Fabrizio signals the
waiter.*

FABRIZIO
I think we need something more festive!
I might even put it on the police bill.

The tuxedo band begins a new round of tunes,
a lively waltz first.

DAVE
On that note, I think we celebrate.
May I, Ms. Katrina, ask you for a dance?

KATE
But —

Dave takes Kate by the hand and leads her into the
space just beyond the tables.
They begin to waltz.

Gradually, other couples join them.
The band responds and plays more loudly.

More couples join, including from outside the Caffè
Qaudri on the other side of the square.

And the band from Quadri also now joins in with the
same waltz.

The camera slowly moves up and back and high
until we see the whole piazza from above,
and it is full of swirling couples.

Hold until:

69. EXT. IN THE ALILAGUNA BOAT GOING TO
THE AIRPORT.

WRITTEN:] Day Seven: Monday.

*Kate and Dave are seated, with Dave's case near
them.*

>   DAVE
> Well, back to the insurance business.
> Could be worse. At least I get to visit Venice
> every so often.

>   KATE
> Thank you for introducing me to it.

>   DAVE
> Not it. Her. *La serenissima.*
> I hope Sarah likes her.

>   KATE
> I asked— and she likes Tintoretto too.

Dave laughs.

70. EXT. IN THE ALILAGUNA BOAT COMING
FROM THE AIRPORT.

*Kate and Sarah are standing in the open part of the
boat, looking at a wonderful sunset as they approach
Venice —*

>   *FADE OUT* .

<u>THE END</u>